BAND
SAW
BENCH
GUIDE

BAND SAW BENCH GUIDE

Mark Duginske

STERLING PUBLISHING CO. INC., NEW YORK

10 9 8 7 6 5 4 3 2 1

Series Editor: Michael Cea
Series Designer: Chris Swirnoff

Published 2002 by Sterling Publishing Company, Inc.
387 Park Avenue South, New York, New York 10016
Originally published under the title *Band Saw: Workshop Bench reference*
© 1999 by Mark Duginske
Distributed in Canada by Sterling Publishing
C/o Canadian Manda Group, One Atlantic Avenue, Suite 105
Toronto, Ontario, Canada M6K 3E7
Distributed in Great Britain and Europe by Cassell PLC
Wellington House, 125 Strand, London WC2R 0BB, England
Distributed in Australia by Capricorn Link (Australia) Pty. Ltd.
P.O. Box 704, Windsor, NSW 2756 Australia

Sterling ISBN 0-8069-9397-9

Acknowledgments

I would like to thank a number of people for helping with this book.

Chris Morris and Laurie Brace, of Page Design Plus,
   did the graphic design work.

Greg Foye from Pinery Imaging
   developed and processed the photos.

Thanks also to:
Laurie Brace, Kate Morris, Mollie Kautza,
and Jim Schwenk for modeling for some of the photos, and
Mike Cea for his work in editing this book.

Contents

Introduction

The band saw is an extremely popular wood-working tool because it can cut a great variety of materials in many different shapes. It is very simple in design, consisting basically of two wheels, a blade, and a table. As the wheels rotate, the blade also rotates and cuts the wood.

Although the band saw is a simple machine with few moving parts, the relationship between these parts is complex. In many ways, it is similar to a musical instrument. Although anyone can make noise with a musical instrument, a pleasant sound will only be achieved if the instrument is tuned properly and the person has the proper skills.

This book is designed to quickly provide information needed to get a pleasing result with the band saw. It is written for band-saw users at all levels of expertise ranging from those who are

Author Mark Duginske.

totally unfamiliar with the tool to experts looking to refine an advanced technique. It explains how the band saw works and the proper way to maintain its parts (Chapter 1); techniques for selecting and using blades, and tracking and maintenance procedures (Chapter 2); band-saw adjustment and alignment methods that help ensure the best possible cut (Chapter 3); techniques for making a wide variety of straight and curved cuts (Chapter 4); how patterns and templates can be used to create interesting designs (Chapter 5); techniques for building and using jigs and fixtures to make an array of cuts (Chapter 6); and the proper safety techniques (Chapter 7). A glossary that follows clarifies any unfamiliar terms.

The information in the following pages is easily accessible. Specific information can be found by referring to the Contents pages, the chapter tabs, the running heads, or index. In certain cases it may be helpful to read the entire chapter, instead of just the specific information, because an overview of all pertinent information may be important. No matter which approach is taken, the reader will find in the following pages ways to make the band saw a more productive and creative workshop companion.

Mark Duginske

Band-Saw Components and Features

Cutting Characteristics of the Band Saw

The band saw is generally defined as a saw blade in the form of an "endless" steel band with teeth on one side that rotates around two or more wheels (1-1). The word endless in this case means that the blade revolves in a continuous cutting motion. The blade, or band, is suspended over two or three metal wheels. As the wheels rotate, so does the blade, which creates the sawing action.

Because the direction of the blade is always downward (1-2), there is no danger that the wood will be thrown back at the operator. This is called kickback. There is always a danger of kickback when a circular saw is being used. For safety reasons, many woodworkers prefer the band saw, especially when cutting small pieces.

One unique feature of the band saw is that the workpiece can be rotated around the blade, creating a curve (1-3). It is the tool most often used when curves have to be cut in wood. If a narrow blade such as a $\frac{1}{16}$-inch blade is being used, the workpiece can be easily rotated around the blade, creating intricate scroll work as shown, in 1-4.

Because the band-saw blade is fairly thin, it can cut thick stock with a minimum of horsepower. For this reason, it is also often used when thick pieces of wood have to be cut or when valuable pieces of wood are made into thin pieces of veneer, as shown in 1-5.

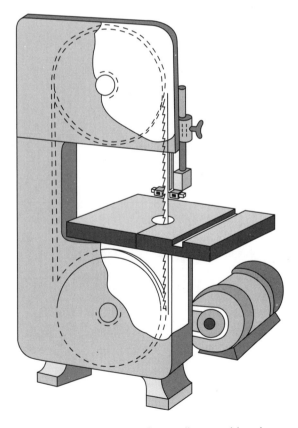

1-1. A band saw consists of an endless steel band with teeth on one side that rotates around two or more metal wheels.

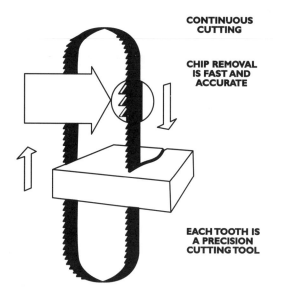

CONTINUOUS CUTTING

CHIP REMOVAL IS FAST AND ACCURATE

EACH TOOTH IS A PRECISION CUTTING TOOL

1-2. The band saw is considered a safe tool to use because the blade has a downward cutting motion. It holds the workpiece on the table.

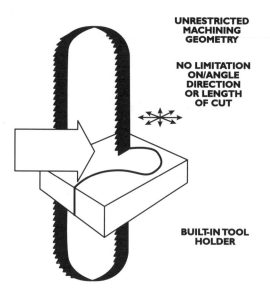

UNRESTRICTED MACHINING GEOMETRY

NO LIMITATION ON/ANGLE DIRECTION OR LENGTH OF CUT

BUILT-IN TOOL HOLDER

1-3. One unique feature of the band saw is that the workpiece can be rotated around the blade, creating a curve.

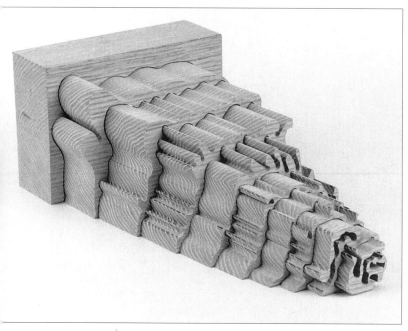

1-4. A 1/16-inch-wide band-saw blade gives a smooth finish in a multigrain cut because the workpiece can be easily rotated around the workpiece. As the blade dulls, the finish becomes smoother. Fine blades last for a fairly long time in oak or other woods which don't contain pitch.

1-5. Resawing oak into veneer with a 3-TPI (teeth per inch) hook-tooth blade. Blades are discussed in Chapter 2.

Band-Saw Classifications

Although band saws come in many different styles, they are generally classified according to the widths of their throats. This is the distance between the blade and the column or post (1-6). For example, a band saw described as a 16-inch band saw has a throat width of 16 inches.

Band saws come with either two or three wheels. The number of wheels a band saw has determines the throat width of the tool. Band saws with three wheels have a large throat width.

Sometimes band saws are classified according to their "depth-of-cut" capacities. This refers to the thickest cut the saw can make. This distance is usually about 6 inches on a consumer-grade saw (1-7). An optional 6-inch height attachment can be bolted between the top and bottom castings of some saws, allowing for the cutting of material up to 12 inches thick.

TWO-WHEEL BAND SAW

THREE-WHEEL BAND SAW

COLUMN

THROAT WIDTH

THROAT WIDTH

1-6. *Band saws are usually classified according to the width of their throats, which is the distance between the blade and the column or post. Notice that the band saw on the right, which has three wheels, has a wider throat capacity than the two-wheel band saw on the left.*

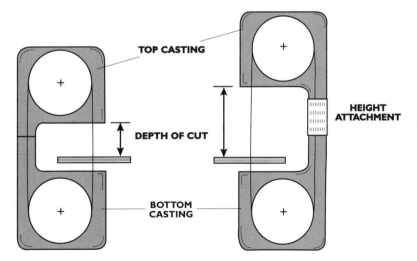

TOP CASTING

HEIGHT ATTACHMENT

DEPTH OF CUT

BOTTOM CASTING

1-7. *Sometimes band saws are classified according to their depth-of-cut capacities, which is the thickest cut the band saw can make.*

Parts and Features

The band saw does not have many parts (1-8). It consists primarily of a frame, cover, table, table slot, trunnions, miter-gauge slot, guide assembly, wheels, and switch. Each part is discussed in the following sections. If not familiar with the band saw, take the time to review the different parts of the band saw shown in 1-8 as they relate to the particular band saw. Even though each manufacturer makes a slightly different machine, the general principles apply.

WHEELS

The blade is suspended over the two wheels. As the wheels rotate, the toothed blade also rotates, creating the downward cutting action. The wheels are usually covered with a piece of rubber called a tire. The tire cushions the blade and protects the teeth from contact with the metal wheel.

The bottom wheel is the drive wheel. It is attached to the power source either directly or through a belt. The bottom wheel powers the

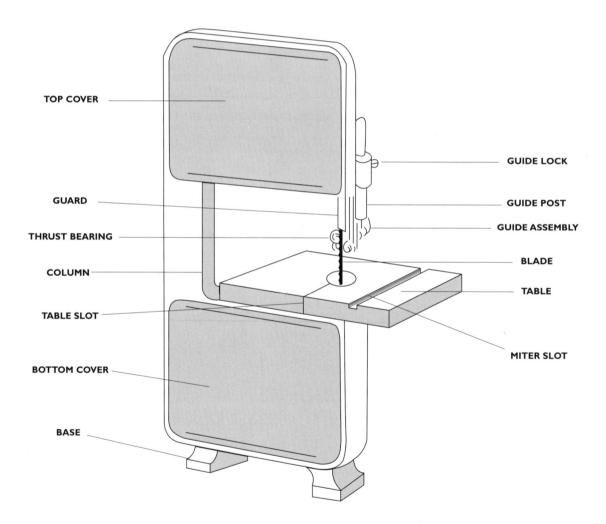

1-8. A typical band saw and its parts. The terms used to describe the different parts sometimes vary. For example, the column is often called a post.

blade and pulls it downward through the workpiece.

The top wheel has two functions, and is adjustable for each one. One function is balancing or tracking the blade on the wheels. The top wheel has an adjustable tilt mechanism that is used to balance the blade. The other function is to tension the blade. The wheel moves upward to increase tension on the blade and downward to decrease the tension.

Refer to Tracking the Blade on pages 68 to 76 for more information.

REPAIRING ECCENTRIC WHEELS

"Eccentric" band-saw wheels are wheels that are not perfectly round or wheels with tires that are not of uniform thickness. Eccentric wheels can cause the band saw to vibrate as the wheels rotate. It is important to check periodically that the wheels are round. If they are not, they have to be trued and then balanced. Each of these steps is described below.

Checking for Wheel Eccentricity

The best time to check for wheel eccentricity is when the blade is on the saw. The metal blade is a better surface to test than the rubber wheel.

The best way to check for wheel eccentricity is with a dial indicator (1-9). There should be not more than .010 inch of variation per wheel. If there is, the wheels are eccentric. Another simple method is to use the guides as a gauge. (See Guide Assembly on page 28.) To do this, loosen the guides so that they move freely. Hold the guides against the blade. Slowly rotate the wheels. If the wheels are eccentric, the blade will move back and forth as the wheels rotate and push the guide away from the blade. After the wheels have been rotated slowly for four or five resolutions, the guides between the space and the

blade should be checked. The more eccentric the wheel, the farther the guides will be pushed away from the blade as the wheel revolves.

If the wheels are only slightly out of round, the blade will move from side to side on the saw. However, if the blade moves more than $\frac{1}{16}$-inch, the blade should be taken off the saw and the cause for the eccentricity further investigated.

A third method of checking that the wheels are round is to clamp a piece of wood to the table and then check the wheels with a feeler gauge (1-10). As with the dial-indicator method, if there is more than .010 inch of variation per wheel, the wheel is eccentric. The next step then is to determine whether the tire or the wheel casting is causing the problem.

Checking the wheel castings on some saws may necessitate the removal of the tires (1-11). On industrial saws, the tires are glued in place and do not have to be removed. On consumer saws, the tires are simply stretched over the rim, and can be easily removed and replaced. This is discussed in detail on pages 22 and 23. Before the tire is removed, both the rim and the tire should be marked, so that the tire can be relocated in its proper position.

If the side-to-side movement of the wheels falls within the normal tolerances, it means that the eccentricity was caused by the tires. As tires wear, they often stretch unevenly and develop thick and thin areas. When this occurs, it is best to order new tires.

Truing Wheels

The two band-saw wheels are never exactly the same size, so they change in proximity to each other. This can cause different vibrations. However, if the wheels are eccentric, the saw will also vibrate as the wheels rotate.

If it is the tires that are eccentric, they will have to be changed. This is not difficult, and is well

1-9. *The best way to check for wheel eccentricity is to use a dial indicator on the blade.*

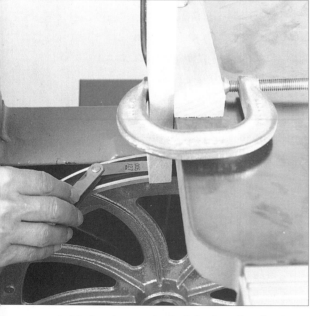

1-10. *Another method of checking for wheel eccentricity is to clamp a wood piece to the table and measure the variation with a feeler gauge.*

1-11. *Checking the wheel casting with a dial indicator.*

within the realm of a woodworker. It is described in Ordering and Installing New Tires on pages 20 and 23. However, truing cast or machined wheels requires metal-working skills and equipment. For this type of work, it is best to contact a machine shop or a motor repair shop.

If the wheels are being trued, it is also worthwhile to have them balanced, if that service is offered. (See the following section on Balancing Wheels.) Once the wheels are turned, the old tires should not be used. A new set should be ordered and installed.

When large industrial saws need tires, the wheels are often sent back to the manufacturer. A new tire is put on the rim and is turned true. The tire is mounted and rotated as if a lathe were being used. A sharp rotating cutting tool cuts off the excess rubber until it is turned true. This is similar to the way tires on a car are turned true. At this point, the tire has had some material removed from the whole surface. No attempt is made to change the wheel. Just the tire is altered.

Balancing Wheels

After the wheels have been trued, they have to be balanced. If the wheels on a band saw are true, yet the top half of the band saw vibrates, it is because the wheels are not balanced. Wheels are unbalanced when one side of the wheel is heavier than the opposite side.

To test for wheel balance, remove the blade and belt. Spin the wheel and let it stop on its own. Mark the bottom of the wheel with a magic marker. Spin the wheel several more times, and then mark the bottom spots with different-colored markers. If all or most of the marks are in one spot, that side of the wheel is the heavy side.

To lighten the heavy side of the wheel, material has to be removed. This is best done with a ¼-inch drill bit. Slowly drill a hole, removing small amounts of material at a time (1-12). Drill the hole in the web of the outside wheel casting rather than the outside rim. After a small amount of material has been removed, spin the wheel again to see if it stops in the same place. If the wheel is badly out of balance and it is large, more than one hole may have to be drilled.

The wheel may have been balanced by the manufacturer once before. Either holes were drilled by the manufacturer or weights were added to the light side of the wheel (1-13). If holes were drilled, the wheel can be rebalanced by drilling additional holes. If the manufacturer used weights, balancing the wheels will be more complicated. The weights often slip loose. The best approach is to take the weights off the wheel completely and start rebalancing from scratch using the testing method described and then drilling the wheels. Although this method sounds tiresome, it only takes minutes and the benefits are well worth the time spent.

1-12. *Lightening the heavy side of a band-saw wheel. This is done by slowly drilling a hole, removing small amounts of material at a time.*

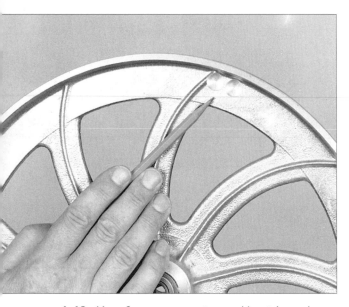

1-13. Manufacturers sometimes add weight to the light side of a wheel.

WHEEL MAINTENANCE TECHNIQUES

The bottom wheel of a band saw should be cleaned regularly, to prevent sawdust from building up on it. This can cause the blade to lead, shorten its life, and cause the band saw to vibrate.

Some band saws have small brushes mounted to them that contact the bottom wheel and help prevent dust buildup (1-14). This is a good way to clean the wheel, and it is advisable to mount a wire or hard bristle brush to a saw that does not have one already mounted to it.

The wheels of the band saw should be occasionally sanded and the tires resurfaced. To resurface the tire, first remove the blade. (Refer to Tire Repair and Maintenance on pages 21 to 23 for more information on tires.) Sanding presents a problem because the top wheel is not powered as is the bottom wheel. The best approach is to use an outside power source such as an electric drill to power the wheel (1-15). Attach a small sanding drum such as a 1¼-inch sanding drum to the drill. An electric drill can be used instead of the saw motor to power the bottom wheel. The drill

1-14. Some manufacturers such as INCA mount a stiff brush on the band saw so that it cleans the bottom wheel. This is advantageous and is a technique that can be used on any band saw.

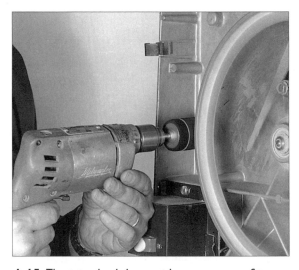

1-15. The top wheel does not have a source of power, so an outside source such as a drill should be used to rotate it. Here a drill is being used with a 1¼-inch sanding drum to rotate the wheel.

can be used at a slower speed. Make sure the blade is not on the band saw when the power is turned on. Use 100- to 120-grit sandpaper to smooth the entire surface.

WHEEL TROUBLESHOOTING TECHNIQUES	The information in this section will help the reader solve problems that occur with band-saw wheels.	
Problem	**Reason**	**Solution**
1. Upper wheel is noisy	Needle bearing is dry or does not turn easily	Regrease the needle bearing
	Bearing is worn or damaged	Replace bearings. It is advisable to have factory-authorized service center do this.
2. Lower wheel is noisy or does not turn easily	Pulley slips on the shaft	Secure pulley. If the pulley is worn, replace it.
	V-belt too tight	Relax the tension on the V-belt
	Shaft bearings worn or damaged	Align the pulley(s) with a straightedge
	Pulleys not aligned	Replace bearings. It is advisable to have a factory-authorized service center do this.

TIRE REPAIR AND MAINTENANCE

Restoring the Tire's Original Shape

The rubber tire on a band-saw wheel acts as a cushion between the blade and the wheels. It acts as a buffer, particularly when the wheels are not truly round. As the tire ages, it has a tendency to stretch, allowing the blade to slip or slide on the wheels. This can have a negative effect on blade tracking and often causes the blade to slide off the wheel. When the blade has tracking problems, a loose tire may be the reason why.

When a tire is used a lot, it will become thin in the middle (1-16). When this happens, the blade will not track well in the middle of the wheel. The reason for this is fairly simple. When a wheel is convex or "crowned," the blade will be pulled automatically toward the crown. It usually will not track exactly in the middle of the crown, but

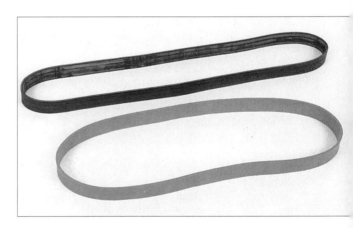

1-16. The top tire has become worn in the middle.

will balance toward the front of the crown. As the tire wears, the crown is worn down, which causes concavity in the tire. If there is a concavity, the blade will track on the front or back half of the wheel, but not in the middle. For this reason, it is important to occasionally restore the original shape of the wheels by sanding the outer edges of the tires so that the middle forms the crown again.

Ordering and Installing New Tires

The tires on a band saw will eventually wear out and new tires will have to be installed. New tires should also be installed when the tires on the band saw have cracked, stretched, or worn thin. Installing new tires is not difficult. Make sure that the tires are at least 1/16-inch thick. Their thickness can be determined by pressing a pin into the tire until it touches the metal wheel.

When tires are replaced, some of the problems that the band saw may have, such as a blade that frequently falls off, are sometimes resolved. New tires will also improve the way a blade tracks and even extend its life. New tires can be ordered through machine dealers and businesses that specialize in tool parts and repairs.

Tires can also be ordered through the parts departments of department stores such as Sears that sell tools. Local tool dealers may have tires on hand. A problem may be encountered if ordering tires for "off-brand" band saws, particularly if the manufacturer has gone out of business. In such a case, the best thing to do is to order a set of tires from a company that sells a saw that's about the size of your saw.

To install a new tire, follow these step-by-step methods:

1. Examine the new tire for defects. Also, allow it to reach room temperature. Never put a cold tire on a saw. A cold tire does not stretch much and is more likely to be brittle and snap.

2. Take the wheel off the saw and remove the old tire. Check the bearings for play. Then clean the wheel as thoroughly as possible with a solvent and a wire brush. (Refer to Cleaning Tires, which follows.)

3. Clamp the tire onto one side of the rim. The tire is very small in comparison to the wheel, so it may have to be stretched a bit to get it on the wheel. Heating the tire in very warm soapy water may make it much easier to stretch. Ivory soap works well.

4. Place a dowel through the wheel hole and into a vise (1-17). This allows access to all sides of the tire and wheel.

5. Stretch the tire over half of the wheel. Then, using a screwdriver or a flat object between the tire and the wheel, stretch the tire until it is on the outside of the wheel (1-18). After the tire is in place, remove the clamp and make sure that the tire is straight. Because the tire may have stretched unevenly over the wheel, it is important that it be stretched evenly. Make several rotations of the screwdriver around the wheel, stretching the tire. This will ensure that the tire is stretched evenly around the wheel. If the old tires were held in place with an adhesive, the new tires should be glued on with tube cement. Use a tube cement that will not soften if exposed to heat. A variety of such cements are usually available in good hardware stores.

Cleaning Tires

It is important that the tires remain clean. This is because as the saw cuts, some sawdust lands between the blade and the bottom wheel. As the blade rotates, the sawdust compresses on the bottom wheel. This is especially true of woods such as pine. The compressed sawdust can have a number of negative effects. It can cause vibration, shorten blade life, and cause the blade to lead.

The best way to clean the tires and maintain their original shapes is to sand them with sandpaper. The surface of an old tire will often harden or glaze over and should be redressed

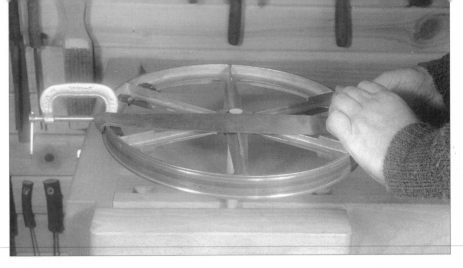

1-17. Clamp a tire on one side of the rim. Then place a dowel through the saw hole. A tapered dowel will work best. Place the dowel in a vise. Press the wheel securely into the dowel. Stretch the tire as far as possible by hand.

1-18. Insert a screwdriver or another flat object without sharp corners between the wheel and the tire. Advance the screwdriver with one hand and secure the tire on the wheel with the other. When the tire is in place around the wheel, before removing the screwdriver rotate it around the wheel several times to stretch the tire evenly around the wheel.

occasionally. This can be done by sanding the wheel with 100-grit sandpaper, ideally with the wheel rotating. This will also remove some of the rubber from the tire and expose a new tire surface, which is desirable.

When touching a rotating wheel with sandpaper, be very careful. Remove the blade first. Never sand the tires with the blade on the machine. Sand the bottom tire with the saw running. It is advisable to first attach the sandpaper to a stick (1-19). Some sandpaper comes with an adhesive-coated back. Sandpaper can also be attached with glue or rubber cement.

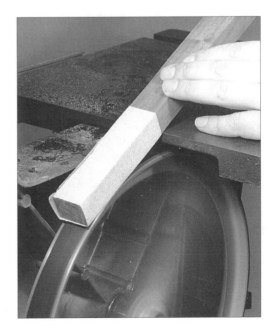

1-19 (right). It is advisable to mount sandpaper on a stick when sanding a band-saw wheel.

FRAME

Most of the important parts of the band saw, including the wheels and table, attach to the frame. There are two general types of frames, but each manufacturer makes the frame differently.

Frames are either one-piece castings or of the skeletal type. A one-piece casting is one large casting that provides both the main framework and the cover for the back of the wheels (1-20). Skeletal frames are simple frameworks that are either cast or welded to the band saw. A separate piece of sheet metal is attached to the frame to safely cover the back of the saw (1- 21). This protective cover is called a wheel housing.

I-20. This Sears band saw has a one-piece casting. This casting provides both the main framework and the cover for the back of the wheels.

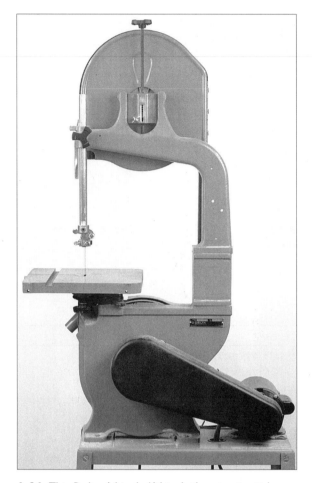

I-21. This Delta 14-inch (14-inch throat capacity) band saw has a skeletal framework, which is either cast or welded to the band saw, and wheel covers.

COVER

Covers protect the operator from the wheels and the blade. If the blade breaks, the pieces of blade are contained by the covers.

The covers are either of one or two pieces. Some are hinged to the band saw (1-22); some are attached with knobs or clips. The two most common materials used for covers are plastic and metal. Plastic is less susceptible to vibration, and does not make as much noise when vibrating. Secure metal covers tightly, to avoid noisy vibration.

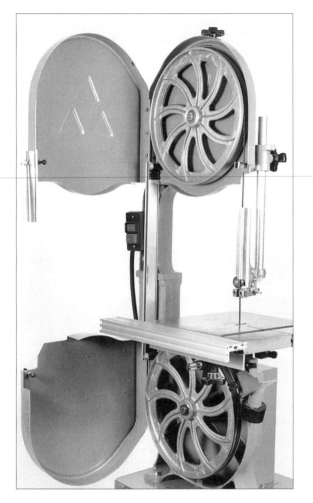

1-22. *The two-piece cover on this band saw is hinged to it. Hinged covers allow easy access to the inside of the band saw.*

TABLE

The workpiece rests on the table as it is fed into the blade. The table surrounds the blade (1-23). A large hole in the middle of the table around the blade, called the table slot (see the section below), allows the operator to make adjustments below the table. This hole is covered by the throat plate. The throat plate is made of either plastic or metal. A plastic plate is quieter and won't cause any damage if the blade accidentally touches it.

TABLE SLOT

A slot in the table allows the blade entry into the middle of the table. There is usually a mechanism to keep the two separated halves of the table in line with each other (1-24). It may be a bolt, a pin, or a screw. Some manufacturers use the front rail to align the two table halves.

Make sure that the saw-table halves are aligned. If not, there is the chance that the two halves will warp in opposite directions, causing an uneven table.

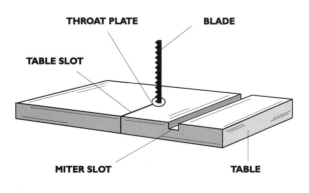

THROAT PLATE   BLADE

TABLE SLOT

MITER SLOT   TABLE

1-23. *The parts of a typical band-saw table.*

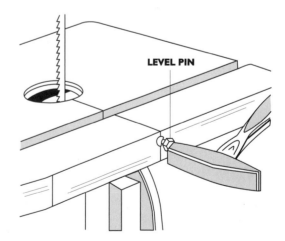

LEVEL PIN

1-24. *Band saws have a mechanism that allows the table to be aligned on each side of the slot. The mechanism for this band saw is a level pin. The pin is gently tapped into the hole, forcing the two sides into proper alignment. To remove the pin, turn it with a wrench.*

TABLE-TILTING FEATURE

The table on most band saws is designed to tilt, which means that it can make beveled or angled cuts. The table tilts away from the column up to 45 degrees (1-25 and 1-26). On some models, it also tilts toward the column up to 10 degrees (1-25). This added feature may be handy at times, but it is not

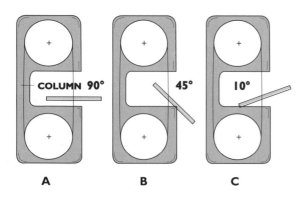

1-25. *The band-saw table on most band saws tilts away from the column up to 45 degrees. On some saws, it also tilts toward the column up to 10 degrees.*

1-26. *A variety of angled or beveled cuts can be made with a tilted table.*

a necessity. It is most useful for cutting dovetail pins on the band saw. (See pages 111 to 122 for information on cutting dovetails.) Underneath the table there is an adjustable bolt or screw to help level the table back to 90 degrees after it has been tilted.

Sears sells a band saw that has a stationary table and a tilting head. This was a common design on large industrial band saws in the past, especially those used for boatbuilding.

TRUNNIONS

The table is attached to two semicircular metal pieces called trunnions (1-27). The trunnion mates with another semicircular piece attached to the bottom of the table. This mechanism allows the table to angle. After the table is adjusted to the desired angle, it is locked in place with the trunnion lock. A scale and a pointer register the angle of tilt. The pointer and the leveling bolt should be adjusted to an accurate 90 degrees. The best way to do this is to use an accurate square (1-28).

1-27. *A close-up of the front trunnion on a band saw. Clean and lubricate the trunnion often if the table is frequently tilted. Avoid grease as a lubricant because it traps sawdust. A lubricant such as Teflon or graphite works well.*

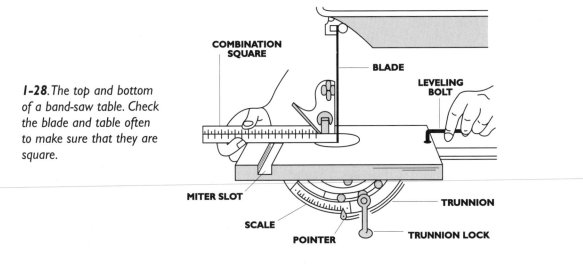

1-28. The top and bottom of a band-saw table. Check the blade and table often to make sure that they are square.

COMBINATION SQUARE

BLADE

LEVELING BOLT

MITER SLOT

SCALE

POINTER

TRUNNION

TRUNNION LOCK

TABLE TROUBLESHOOTING TECHNIQUES

The information in this section will help the reader solve problems that occur with band-saw tables.

Problem	Reason	Solution
1. Table not properly aligned	Table is not secure	Secure tilt lock and trunnion bolt as described
2. Table not tilted, as indicated by pointer	Scale out of alignment	Square table at 90 degrees to the blade and readjust the scale.
3. Table not flat	Warped table	Shim the table from underneath. The trunnion may have pulled the table out of alignment. If this doesn't work, replace the table.
4. Table hard to tilt	Sawdust trapped between base and trunnion	Clean trunnion and table slot in the base. The table may have to be removed. Lubricate the table trunnion with a dry lubricant. Don't use oil or grease because it attracts dust.
	Metal burrs on trunnion	Remove burrs with file or sandpaper. The table may have to be removed.
5. Table insert contacts the blade	Poor alignment from the factory	File the table insert.
	Table inset is turned around	Turn the insert around
6. Workpiece does not slide easily on the table	Dirt or pitch on the table	Clean and wax table. If pitch is the problem, remove it with mineral spirits.
	Table insert too high	If insert is bent, try to straighten it (1-29). If not, replace it. Sand or file its back down.
	Dirt under the table insert	Clean the area under the table insert

MITER-GAUGE SLOT

Most saws have a miter-gauge slot (1-29). This slot runs parallel to the blade and accepts the miter-gauge bar, which is usually used for cross-cutting (cutting across the grain of the wood). The miter-gauge slot is very helpful for when user-made jigs are being employed. Many jigs are designed to operate parallel to the blade, and the miter-gauge slot provides the most logical path.

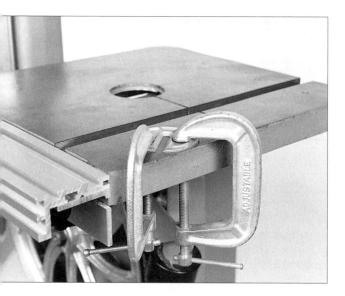

1-29. Straightening a bent table insert. Notice the miter-gauge slot, a feature on most band saws.

GUIDE ASSEMBLY

There are two guide assemblies which support the blade. One is located below the table, and one above the table. The top assembly is attached to a metal rod called the guide post (1-30).

The entire upper guide assembly is adjustable up and down, so it can be adjusted just above the workpiece (1-31). The guide-post lock screw locks the post at the desired height. The blade guard is attached to the front of the guide post.

Each guide assembly consists of two guide blocks or bearings that are located on each side

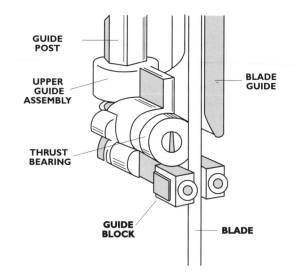

1-30. A close-up of the upper guide assembly.

of the blade and keep it from twisting. Each assembly also houses the thrust bearing, which keeps the blade from being pushed rearwards when the saw is cutting.

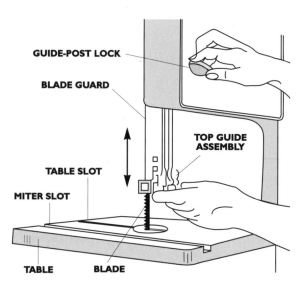

1-31. The upper guide assembly is adjustable up and down. The blade guard, which protects the operator from the blade, is attached to the front of the assembly. For safety and performance reasons, the assembly should be locked approximately 1/4 inch above the workpiece.

REMOVING AND REPLACING THRUST BEARINGS AND GUIDE BLOCKS

Thrust bearings can become worn or scarred (1-32). Some can be removed from the shaft and reversed, thus providing a new surface. Check the rotation of the bearings frequently. If they do not rotate easily, they should be replaced. New bearings should be ordered from the dealer or the manufacturer of the band saw.

Guide blocks can also wear out and become rounded. Cool Blocks, nonmetallic guide blocks, wear out slightly faster than the metal guides. Both types of blocks should be resurfaced as needed.

Resurface the blocks with a file, power disc, or a belt sander.

1-32. The bearing on the left is new. The bearing in the middle has a scar on the top of it. The bearing on the right is completely destroyed. This bearing was under the table and was covered with pin pitch, which prevented it from rotating efficiently.

GUIDE AND THRUST-BEARING TROUBLESHOOTING TECHNIQUES	The information in this section will help the reader solve problems that occur with band-saw guides and thrust bearings.	
Problem	**Reason**	**Solution**
1. Upper guide post hard to adjust	Post needs to be cleaned	Clean post and lubricate with graphite *1-33.* Cleaning the guide post using graphite.
2. Guides not parallel to blade	Guides worn or damaged	Resurface guides with sandpaper or file them. One option is to replace old metal blocks with non-metallic blocks.
	Guides not aligned properly	Resurface and realign guide blocks
	Blade twists in guides	Guides set too far apart. When turning corners, use light pressure. Do not twist blade without simultaneously moving workpiece forward.
3. Thrust bearing damaged or scarred	Thrust-bearing surface has scars and ridges	Reverse bearing by pressing it off shaft. If bearing is not reversible, replace entire unit.
	Thrust bearing makes squealing noise	Bearing is damaged and should be replaced. Replace only the bearing unit if possible.

SWITCH

The band-saw motor is turned on and off with a switch. On some models, the switch is attached to the saw. On other models, it is on the stand.

There are safety devices designed on some switches. The Sears band saw, for example, has a removable plastic key to discourage unauthorized use of the saw.

If children may be tempted to turn on the band saw, make sure some kind of protection is used. A locked electrical panel will protect the entire shop.

Machine Troubleshooting Techniques

A band-saw operator may encounter several problems when using a band saw. These problems range from basic problems such as a machine that will not start to vibration problems to overloaded motors. These problems and others are discussed below.

VIBRATION

Band saws have a tendency to vibrate more than other power tools. This can be very frustrating because it is difficult and fatiguing to do a good job on such a machine. Vibration also affects the quality of the cut.

Many different band-saw components or combination of components can cause vibration. This includes the motor, pulley, belt, saw shaft, wheels, tires, and blade. It is best to try to isolate the part causing the vibration, using a systematic approach. Check one part at a time. First take the blade off the saw, and then take the belt off the motor. Run the motor to see if it vibrates. If it does, take the pulley off and see how the motor runs without it. If it vibrates without the pulley,

it has to be determined if it is the motor or the setup on the saw that is causing the vibration. Take the motor off the saw. If it vibrates off the saw, it should be repaired or replaced with a new motor.

If the motor doesn't vibrate off the saw but does on the saw stand, the cause of the vibration may be the stand. Consider building a new wood stand. If it is a metal stand that is causing the vibration, reinforce it with plywood.

If the motor and stand do not vibrate until the pulley is attached, a new pulley is needed. The average band saw comes with a cheap cast pulley. To ensure good performances of the band saw, the cheap cast pulley should be replaced with a new machined steel pulley.

Even if the source of the vibration is the pulley and it has been replaced with a good-quality one, there may still be some slight vibration. This can often be controlled by mounting a rubber pad under the motor or the saw. One such pad is a polymer that is available under the name Visc-Elastic. This black rubbery material, patented by a British company, is designed to absorb shock and dampen vibration. A layer of this material is used on top of and underneath the band saw and/or motor (1-34). When this material is used on the saw and the motor, a significant amount of vibration can be eliminated. If this material is not available, a rubber floor mat can be used. Rubber washers may be available in the plumbing departments of hardware stores.

If the source of vibration has not yet been determined, next attach the belt and turn on the machine. If there is vibration, this indicates that the saw pulley, belt, or saw shaft is the cause.

Determining which of these three parts is the reason for the vibration takes some work. Start by replacing the belt because this is cheaper than buying a new, large machined pulley. Next, check the pulley by holding a

1-34. A rubber pad placed under the motor or the saw can dampen band-saw vibration.

piece of wood against it and rotating the pulley by hand.

If both the belt and the pulley are okay, the shaft may be causing the vibration. Take off the bottom wheel and run the band saw. Determine if the shaft is moving in an eccentric fashion by turning the saw off and watching the shaft when it slows down. Rotate the shaft and measure it by holding a piece of wood against it. This procedure, called "checking the middle of the machine," often doesn't work if the shaft has a keyway slot. Another option is to use a dial indicator if one is available.

After the "bottom" and the "middle" of the band saw have been checked, the next step is to check the "top" of the machine. This consists of checking the band saw with the bottom wheel attached but without a blade. Turn the machine on and observe the bottom wheel. Is there more vibration? Does the wheel appear to run eccentrically as the saw slows down?

The roundness of the wheel can be checked with a dial indicator if one is available. Another method is to hold a piece of wood against the wheel and feel if the wood moves as the wheel is rotated by hand (1-35). A way to determine roughly how much the wheel is out-of-round is to place the stick on the support and rest it against the wheel. Then slowly turn the wheel by hand. A gap will appear between the stick and the wheel as it rotates. The bigger the gap, the more eccentric the wheel.

The next step is to check the eccentricity of the top wheel. This can also be done with a support piece and a stick if a dial indicator is available.

The final step consists of running the saw with the blade on. If vibration increases when the saw runs with the blade on, there is a good chance that the wheels are eccentric or unbalanced. If this is the case, refer to pages 17 to 20.

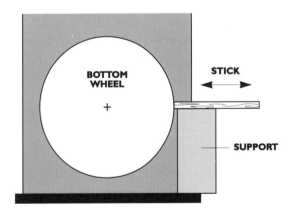

1-35. One way to check the roundness of a wheel is to hold a piece of wood against the wheel and feel if the wood moves as the wheel is rotated by hand.

MACHINE TROUBLESHOOTING TECHNIQUES

The information in this section will help the reader solve problems that occur with band saws.

Problem	Reason	Solution
1. Band saw will not start	Band saw not plugged in	Plug the band saw in
	Fuse blown or circuit breaker tripped	Replace fuse or reset breaker
	Cord damaged	Replace the cord
	Overload relay not set	Replace reset button on motor
	Defective motor	Replace or rebuild motor
	Defective motor capacitor	Replace capacitor
	Band saw stiff from the cold	Warm shop up to at leat 55 degrees Fahrenheit
2. Motor over-loaded and cuts out frequently	Low current	Put saw on a higher circuit or contact electrician
	Material fed too fast	Feed material more slowly
	Extension cord too light or long	Replace with adequate cord
3. Band saw does not come up to full speed	Low circuit current	Use higher circuit or consult electrician
	Extension cord too light or long	Replace with adequate cord
	Motor not wired for correct voltage or wiring	Refer to motor nameplate for wiring diagram. This is usually on the motor.
	Motor wired incorrectly	Rewire motor following wire diagram
4. Motor runs in wrong direction	Motor wired incorrectly	Rewire motor following wire diagram
5. Crooked sawing	Blade tension too low	Increase blade tension to recommended amount
	Guides and bearings poorly adjusted	Properly readjust bearings and guides as described
	Dull blade	Have blade sharpened or replace blade
	Blade pitch is too fine	Use blade with coarser pitch (fewer teeth per inch)
	Damaged blade teeth	Replace blade
	Fence poorly aligned	Realign fence

Selecting a Blade

Although band saw blades all have the same basic design, they each have their own particular cutting characteristics (2-1). To get the best possible cut, it is important that a blade with characteristics best suited for the given task be used. For example, a very coarse blade will cut like a chain saw, and a very fine blade will allow the band saw user to do very intricate scroll work. Also, using a blade for its intended purpose allows for maximum efficiency when cutting and is the best way to prolong its usable life. Conversely, if the wrong blade is used for a particular application, its life can be shortened and its teeth dulled.

There are a huge quantity of blades available that

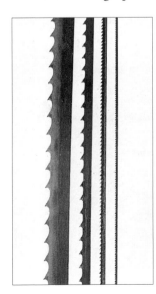

have various combinations of different characteristics relating to width, type thickness, pitch, and set of teeth, all of which are discussed in the following sections. This is an advantage. If the band saw operator has five different blades in the

2-1. *A variety of band-saw blades.*

workshop rather than a couple, there is a better chance the proper blade for the specific work will be available. The following section on Width, Form, and Pitch will help woodworkers determine what type of blade is best suited for a specific cutting situation. Width, form, and pitch are the three blade characteristics that play the most important part in the blade's cutting performance.

WIDTH, PITCH, AND FORM: THE THREE MOST IMPORTANT BLADE CHARACTERISTICS

A blade's width, pitch, and form determine how successfully the blade will make certain cuts. There are several factors that determine what to look for in a blade regarding width, pitch, and form. Depending on the cutting situation, some of these factors will be more important than others. They are:

1. The orientation of the grain, that is whether crosscuts (cuts across the grain), rip cuts (cuts with the grain), or multigrain cuts (rip and crosscuts) are being made. See Tooth Set and Form on pages 38 to 41 for more information on selecting the blade with the proper set and form to make crosscuts, rip cuts, or multigrain cuts.

2. Whether the material being cut is hard or soft. As a general rule, remember that the harder the material, the finer the pitch that is required for a blade. Refer to Material Hardness and Proper

Pitch on page 37 for more information on selecting a blade with the proper pitch for cutting specific material.

3. Tightness of curves. This will determine the width of the blade. Refer to Blade Width, which follows this section, for information on curve tightness and blade width.

4. Speed of cut.

5. Smoothness of cut. Refer to Standard-Tooth Blades on page 38 for information on the best blade to use when smoothness is a priority.

6. Accuracy of cut.

7. Straightness of cut.

8. Depth of cut.

Blade width is the first characteristic that should be considered. If all of the cuts in the work will be straight cuts, a wide blade should be used for added beam strength. If there are curves, determine blade width by how many curves there are and how large they are.

The next determination when choosing a blade is its pitch. The pitch of a blade is usually indicated by the number of teeth per inch a blade has. This is referred to as TPI (Teeth Per Inch). A coarse blade has few teeth. A fine blade has many teeth. The coarser the blade, the faster the cut. Refer to Pitch on page 36 for more information.

The third determination when choosing a blade is its form and set. The form is the shape of the teeth. Set is the reference to the bend of the teeth. (Refer to Tooth Form and Set on pages 38 to 41 for more information.) This is determined by the orientation of the grain. Choosing the tooth form also affects the blade's pitch. A blade with standard-teeth form has twice as many teeth as blade with other forms.

The following sections contain information on width, form and pitch that will allow the reader

to make an educated decision when choosing a blade for a specific application.

Blade Width

Blades are usually classified according to their widths, which is the measurement from the back of the blade to the front of the teeth. The width of the blade determines how tight a turn the blade can make. The narrower the blade, the tighter the turn (2-2). The wider the blade, the more likely it is to resist deflection. For this rea-

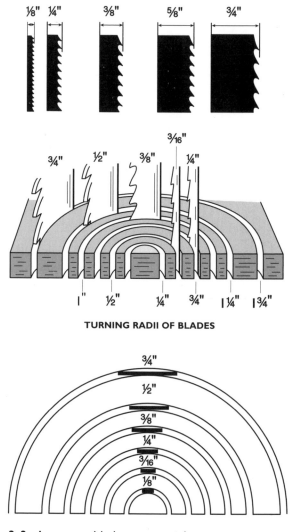

TURNING RADII OF BLADES

2-2. A narrow blade can cut tighter curves.

son, wider blades are preferred over narrow blades when straight cuts are being made.

A ½-inch blade is the widest blade that is practical to use on a consumer-grade band saw. Some owners' manuals claim that a ¾-inch blade can be used, but do not use a blade this wide on a saw that has wheels less than 18 inches in diameter. A ¼-inch blade is the most frequently used blade for general-purpose work.

For years, the narrowest blade that was available was the ⅛-inch blade. This blade will make a turn about the size of a pencil eraser. However, ¹⁄₁₆-inch blades are now available. A ¹⁄₁₆-inch blade will make a 90-degree turn. This very small blade requires special nonmetal guide blocks called Cool Blocks.

Refer to Scroll-Sawing on pages 92 and 93 for more information on cutting with ¹⁄₁₆-inch blades.

Determining Blade Width Using a Radius Chart

The amount and size of the detail in a pattern will determine the blade width. Choose as wide a blade as possible, yet one that will make the tightest curves with ease. To determine the size of the blade's width, determine the smallest curve in the pattern and match the blade to that radius.

Until the band-saw user is well acquainted with the saw, it is best to use the contour (radius) chart shown in 2-3 to determine which width of blade to cut a specific radius. Radius charts can be found in many woodworking books and magazine articles and on blade boxes. They differ slightly from one another, but are good as general indicators of how tightly a curve can be cut with a particular blade.

If a blade is matched with a curve on the chart, the blade can cut that curve without backtracking. For example, a ³⁄₁₆-inch blade will cut a circle with a ⁵⁄₁₆-inch radius.

There are options to matching the blade to the smallest curve in the pattern. If there is only one very tight cut, it may be best to use a turning hole, a relief cut, or successive passes, or to change the blade. If many curves are being cut, the band-saw operator can use a wider blade for the larger curves and then switch to a narrower blade for the tighter curves. Changing blades can often save cutting and finishing time.

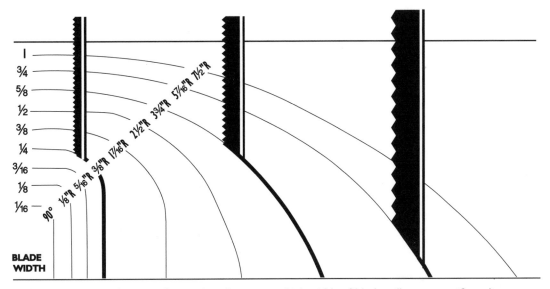

2-3. This radius chart can be used to determine which width of blade will cut a specific radius.

Determining Blade Width
Using Coins or a Pencil

Coins or a pencil can also be used to determine which width of blade to use. A quarter is the size of the tightest cut that can be made with a ¼-inch blade. A dime is the size of the tightest curve that can be cut with a ³⁄₁₆-inch blade. A pencil eraser is the size of the tightest turn that can be made with a ⅛-inch blade. After a while, the band-saw user won't even need these objects to determine the size of blade for the curve. He or she will be able to do it simply by sight.

Pitch

Pitch is a term that refers to the size of the teeth on the blade. It is usually given in a number that indicates how many teeth are in one inch of blade,

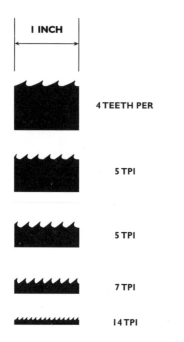

2-4. *A blade's pitch is measured by the number of teeth it has per inch (TPI). It is common for wide blades to have fewer teeth than narrow blades, which often have many teeth. If a blade has fewer teeth per inch, that is, has a pitch that is too coarse, the teeth will dull prematurely.*

generally referred to as TPI (Teeth per Inch) (2-4). The words "coarse" and "fine" are used to describe the number of teeth in a blade. A coarse blade has few teeth. A fine blade has many teeth. The coarser the blade, the faster the cut.

It is important that the pitch of the blade be matched to the material that is being cut. There should be at least three teeth in the material at any given time during the saw cut. A blade with more teeth will give a smoother cut, but one with too many teeth will create other problems, such as cutting slowly or building up excessive heat (2-5). Excessive heat shortens the life of the blade because it causes the teeth to dull quickly. It also shortens the life of the blade.

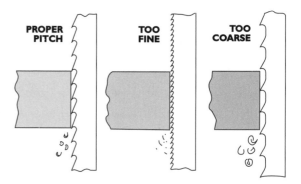

2-5. *A blade with the proper pitch is essential to making the most efficient cut.*

Variable-Pitch Blades

A variable-pitch blade has been developed for the metal-cutting industry. This blade is designed to decrease vibration on interrupted cuts such as tubing, U-channels, and I beams where excessive vibration is a problem. It can also be used to cut solid bar stock.

The size of the teeth on variable-pitch blades progressively change in size from large and small and back to large again (2-6). The blade is designed so that it dampens vibration. Woodworking variable-

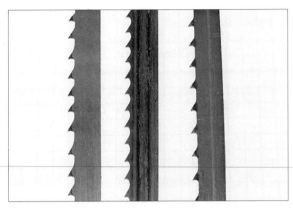

2-6. The variable-pitch blade was developed to cut structural shapes. It is used to cut thicker stock and to resaw, that is to cut a board in half along its width.

pitch blades are used to cut thicker stock and to resaw, that is to cut a board in half along its width.

Material Hardness and Proper Pitch

When choosing a blade with the proper pitch, one factor that should be considered is the hardness of the material that is being cut (2-7). The harder the material, the finer the pitch that is required. For example, exotic hardwoods such as ebony and rosewood require blades with a finer pitch than American hardwoods such as oak and maple. Softwood such as pine is best cut with a blade that is fairly coarse. If the blade has too

DETERMINING PROPER PITCH

When using a blade to make a cut, there are certain conditions that will indicate if the pitch of the blade is correct for the job or whether the blade is too fine or too coarse. They are listed below:

Proper Pitch

1. The blade cuts quickly.
2. A minimum amount of heat is created when the blade cuts.
3. Minimum feeding pressure is required.
4. Minimum horsepower is required.
5. The blade makes quality cuts for a long period.

Pitch That Is Too Fine

1. The blade cuts slowly.
2. There is excessive heat, which causes the blade to break prematurely or dull rapidly.
3. Unnecessarily high feeding pressure is required.
4. Unnecessarily high horsepower is required.
5. The blade wears excessively.

Pitch That Is Too Coarse

1. The blade has a short cutting life.
2. The teeth wear excessively.
3. The band saw vibrates.

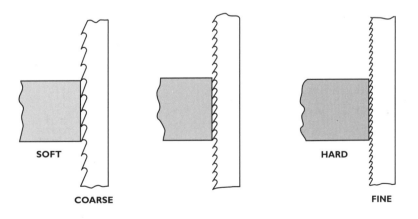

SOFT

COARSE

HARD

FINE

2-7. Hard material requires blades with a finer pitch than those used to cut soft material.

many teeth, the pitch in the pine will quickly clog it, decreasing its ability to cut. Having blades of the same width with a variety of tooth configurations will most likely provide an acceptable quantity of blades to choose for a particular job (2-8). Two hook-tooth blades with 30 TPI are recommended. Two skip-tooth blades, one having 4 TPI and the other 6, are good for general-purpose work. One-eighth-inch-wide blades with 10 and 14 TPI will handle most crosscutting and tight-turn work.

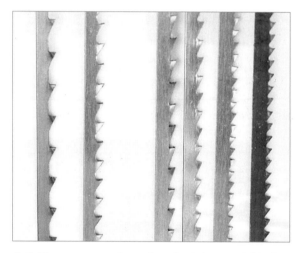

2-8. There are a variety of tooth pitches available for each width of blade. The blades shown here are ⅛ inch wide. The blades on the left have a regular-tooth form, and the one on the right has a skip-tooth form.

Tooth Form and Set

The teeth on a blade come in one of two shapes. If the face of the tooth is 90 degrees to the body of the blade, it is called a 0-degree rake. If it has a slight positive angle, it is called a hook tooth (2-9).

A blade with 0-degree rake cuts with a scraping action. This makes a smooth cut, but increases heat caused by the cutting. A blade with hook teeth cuts more aggressively. It makes a rougher cut, but less heat is generated, which means that the blade can be used for a longer period of time.

Types of Blades with Different Forms

Blades can be broken down into three general groups according to the form of their teeth. These blades are called standard-tooth blades, skip-tooth blades, and hook-tooth blades. They are discussed below.

Standard-Tooth Blades A blade with standard teeth has teeth spaced closely together (2-9). It has a 0-degree rake and makes a very smooth cut. It is the best blade to use to crosscut, to cut small details, to cut diagonally, for multigrain cutting, and when smoothness is a priority because it doesn't tear the wood as it cuts. When thick stock is being cut with a standard-tooth blade, the stock should be fed slowly. Standard-tooth blades are ideal for joinery such as tenons or dovetails.

Skip-Tooth Blades The teeth on skip-tooth blades, like the teeth on standard-tooth blades, have a 0-degree rake (2-9). However, every

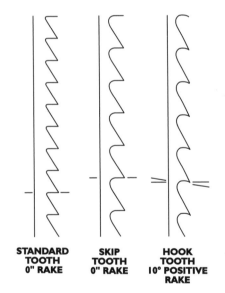

STANDARD TOOTH 0" RAKE   SKIP TOOTH 0" RAKE   HOOK TOOTH 10° POSITIVE RAKE

2-9. Standard and skip teeth have a 0-degree rake angle. Rake angle is the angle of the tooth face as it relates to the tooth back. Hook teeth have a positive angle, which is usually 10 degrees.

other tooth on a skip-tooth blade is removed. Thus, this blade has only half as many teeth as a standard-tooth blade. Because a skip-tooth blade has a coarse pitch, it cuts much faster, especially when the blade is used to cut with the grain (rip cut).

A skip-tooth blade is best suited for cutting long, gentle curves with the grain, and it is acceptable when making multigrain cuts. Although it doesn't cut against the grain as well as a standard-tooth blade or with the grain as well as a hook-tooth blade, it is often the most widely used blade because it provides the best compromise. A ¼-inch-wide skip-tooth blade with 4 to 6 teeth per inch is usually considered the best all-around blade.

Hook-Tooth Blade A hook-tooth blade is the most aggressive blade (2-9). This is because it has a positive rake angle and the fewest number of teeth. It is particularly efficient at cutting thick stock with the grain. It is often acceptable when making multigrain cuts. This makes it the best choice for making straight rip cuts, which are cuts along the grain of wood, and resawing, cutting a board in half throughout its width.

Refer to Rip Cuts and Resawing on pages 98 to 104 for more information on hook-tooth blades.

Tooth Set

The teeth on a band-saw blade are bent or "set" sideways. Thus, the saw kerf (cut) is wider than the body of the blade. Set makes it easier for the band-saw operator to rotate the workpiece around the blade when creating a curved cut. The side clearance of the blade created by the set of teeth also serves to decrease the friction between the blade and the workpiece on straight cuts (2-10).

Blades With Different Tooth Sets

Band-saw blades are available in three basic types of tooth set: alternate set, raker set, and wavy set. Each is described below.

Blades with Alternate-Set Teeth Blades with alternate-set teeth have every other tooth bent in the same direction. A blade with alternate-set teeth makes the most cuts per inch, and thus gives the smoothest cut. This design is most often used on standard- and skip-tooth blades. Blades with this design are well suited for crosscutting.

Blades With Raker-Set Teeth Raker-set teeth are similar to alternate-set teeth except that some of the teeth, called rakers, are not set or bent. Rakers clean the middle of the cut, and are found most often on skip- and hook-tooth blades. This design increases the efficiency of the cutting action, but it decreases the smoothness of the cut because fewer teeth are cutting the side of the kerf. It is often used in conjunction with a hook-

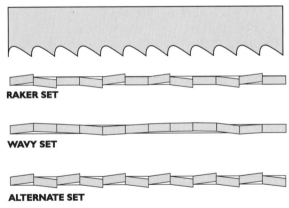

RAKER SET

WAVY SET

ALTERNATE SET

SET STYLES

2-10. Set refers to the bend of the teeth on the blade. It is measured at the widest point of the blade. The three most common set styles are raker, wavy, and alternate set. Alternate-set teeth are all bent in the same direction. Raker-set teeth are actually not set or bent. Wavy-set teeth are alternatively set in opposite directions.

BLADE-SELECTION CHART

Refer to the following chart to determine what width, form, and pitch characteristics to look for in a blade when making specific cuts and cutting different types of material. The proper blade speed and feed rate are also given.

Type of Cut	Pitch	Width	Form	Blade Speed	Feed Rate
Resawing	Coarse	Wide	Hook	Medium or Fast	Slow
Ripping (less than 2")	Medium	Wide	Hook	Slow to Medium	Medium or Fast
Ripping (more than 2")	Coarse	Wide	Hook	Medium or Fast	Slow
Crosscutting (1"or less)	Fine	Wide	Standard	Medium or Fast	Slow
Crosscutting (1"or more)	Medium or Fine	Wide	Standard	Medium or Fast	Slow
Miter Cut	Medium or Fine	Wide	Standard	Medium or Fast	Slow
Tenons	Medium	Medium or wide	Standard	Medium or Fast	Slow to Medium
Round Stock (Ripping)	Medium	Medium or wide	Standard	Medium or Fast	Slow
Round Stock (Crosscut)	Medium or fine	Medium or wide	Standard	Medium	Slow
Sharp Curves	Fine	Narrow	Standard	Slow	Slow
Gradual Curves	Medium or Fine	Medium	Skip	Medium or Slow	Slow to Medium

Type of Material	Pitch	Width	Blade Speed	Feed Rate
Foam:				
Hard	Medium	Medium or wide	Medium or fast	Fast
Soft	(Knife)		Medium	Medium
Rubber:				
Hard	Fine or Medium	Medium	Slow	Slow
Soft	Fine	Medium	Slow	Slow
Bone	Fine or Medium	Medium	Medium	Slow to Medium
Plywood:				
3/4"	Medium	Medium	Medium	Slow to Medium
Less than 1/2"	Fine	Medium	Medium	Slow to Medium
Masonite	Fine or Medium	Medium	Medium	Medium
Plastic:				
Thick	Coarse	Medium	Slow	Slow
Thin	Fine or Medium	Medium	Slow	Slow
Non-Ferrous Metal	Fine	Medium or Wide	Slow	Slow
Paper or Cardboard	Fine	Medium or Wide	Medium	Slow to Medium

Blade Speed:
Slow = 88 ft/minute
Medium = 1800 ft/minute

Feed Rate of Stock:
Slow = 2 ft/min to 4 ft/minute
Medium = 5 ft/minute to 11 ft/minute

tooth design. This combination is very efficient at removing material, and, therefore, useful for resawing.

Blades With Wavy-Set Teeth A blade that has teeth with a wavy set has groups of teeth that are alternately set in opposite directions. This type of set is also used on the handheld hacksaw, and is designed for cutting metal. A variable-pitch blade may have a variable or wavy set which helps to decrease vibration caused by the running blade (2-11). This design is used almost exclusively in the metal-working industry.

CHOOSING SMALL, MEDIUM, AND LARGE BLADES

Band-saw blades are usually classified into three different groups: small, medium, and large (2-12). Their width, tooth form, and pitch determine the group into which they are classified.

Small blades usually have a standard (regular) tooth form and a fine pitch. These blades are good for cutting tight curves. Medium blades usually have a skip-tooth form, a raker set, and a medium-to-coarse pitch. These are good general-purpose blades. Larger blades often have a hook-

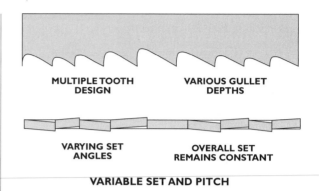

MULTIPLE TOOTH DESIGN   **VARIOUS GULLET DEPTHS**

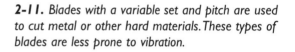

VARYING SET ANGLES   **OVERALL SET REMAINS CONSTANT**

VARIABLE SET AND PITCH

2-11. Blades with a variable set and pitch are used to cut metal or other hard materials. These types of blades are less prone to vibration.

tooth form, a raker set, and a coarse pitch. These blades are most useful for ripping and resawing. It is best to have at least one blade from each group, in order to be prepared for any situation.

Not every blade can be so neatly classified, however. Consider the example of a ½-inch blade with a pitch of 14 TPI (teeth per inch), a standard-tooth form, and an alternate set. This blade is large, yet its teeth are those that are normally found on a blade classified as "small." This blade is often used for cutting metal.

See the following chart for the characteristics of each group of blade.

2-12. Blades are usually divided into three groups: small, medium, and large. Small blades usually have a standard-tooth form and a fine pitch. Medium blades usually have a skip-tooth form, a raker set, and a medium-to-coarse pitch. Large blades often have a hook-tooth form, a raker set, and a coarse pitch.

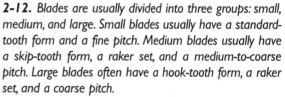

BLADE WIDTH   **MEDIUM RADIUS**

½"
⅜"   3"
¼"   1"
³⁄₁₆"   ⅝"
⅛"   ⅜"
³⁄₁₆"

LARGE BLADES

MEDIUM BLADES

SMALL BLADES

HOOK SKIP   **SKIP/ STANDARD**   **STANDARD**

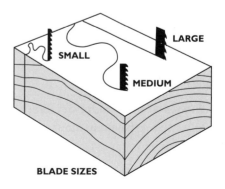

SMALL   **LARGE**

MEDIUM

BLADE SIZES

CHARACTERISTICS OF SMALL, MEDIUM, AND LARGE BLADES	Small	Medium	Large
Width	1/16 – 1/8 Inch	3/16 – 3/8 Inch	1/2 Inch and Over
Pitch	14–32 TPI (fine)	4–12 TPI	2–4 TPI (Coarse)
Tooth	Standard	Standard, Skip, Hook	Hook
Form	0-Degree	0-Degree	10-Degree Positive Hook

OVERVIEW OF BLADE-SELECTION INFORMATION

The blades in this section are grouped according to the preceding information. Refer to this section when determining which blade to use:

Blades Grouped by Type of Form:

1. *Standard-Tooth Blades.* Blades with teeth spaced closely together. They are suited for use when smoothing is a priority or when crosscutting, cutting small details, cutting diagonally, or for multigrain cutting. Usually, these are smaller blades. (See chart above.)

2. *Skip-Tooth Blades.* Blades in which every other tooth is removed. They are best-suited for cutting curves with the grain and are acceptable for making multigrain cuts. These are usually 3/16 to 3/8 inch. (See chart above.)

3. *Hook-Tooth Blades.* Blades with the fewest number of teeth, and, consequently, the most aggressive blades. These blades are best suited for making straight rip cuts and resawing. (See chart above.)

Blades Grouped by Set:

1. *Blades with Alternate-Set Teeth.* Blades with every other tooth bent in the same direction. They are well-suited to crosscutting.

2. *Blades with Raker-Set Teeth.* Blades with some teeth bent in the same directions, and others not bent at all. They are best suited for ripping and crosscutting.

3. *Blades with Wavy-Set Teeth.* Blades with groups of teeth alternately set in opposite directions. They are best suited for metal-cutting.

4. *Variable-Pitch Blades.* Blades with a variable or wavy set designed to decrease vibration when making interrupted cuts in metal.

Blades Grouped By Classification:

1. *Small Blades.* Generally have a standard-tooth form, an alternate set, and a fine pitch. Smaller blades are best suited to tight turns and crosscutting.

2. *Medium Blades.* Generally have a skip-tooth form, a raker set, and a medium-to-coarse pitch. They are best suited for general-purpose work.

3. *Large Blades.* Generally have a hook-tooth form, a raker set, and a coarse pitch. They are best suited for cutting thin stock and making straight cuts.

Special-Purpose Blades

There are a number of blades, sometimes also referred to as bands, that are designed to cut a particular type of material or to make a specific type of cut (2-13). Below are descriptions of those blades that may prove useful in a woodworker's shop.

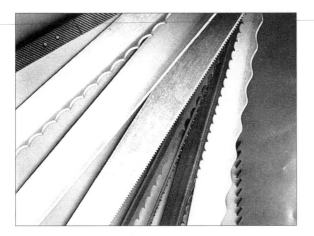

2-13. *There are number of blades made for one specific purpose. Most of these are blades that are used in the industrial sector.*

PLY-CORE BAND

This band is designed specifically to cut plywood, especially thick stacks of plywood. It is thick (.032 to .042 inch thick) and must be used on large band saws. A ply-core band has coarse teeth with hard tips and a flexible back.

FURNITURE BAND

As the name implies, this blade is used by furniture manufacturers to smoothly cut contours and shapes. Most have hard edges and are flexback bands. These blades usually have hook-skip teeth. They either have alternate-set teeth or a raker tooth for every fifth or seventh tooth.

Furniture bands are available in widths of ¼, ⅜, and ½ inch.

FRICTION BAND

The friction band is used in a technique called friction-sawing. Friction-sawing is a unique metal-cutting technique in which the blade runs very fast, up to 15,000 FPM (feet per minute) (2-14). It is a technique that is used to cut composite or complex materials such as high-strength steels, gratings, and screens. Thin material or odd-shaped metal may be friction-sawed when conventional methods fail.

Friction bands are designed for very large saws, because blade length is important for dissipating heat. The high speed of the blade creates heat, which melts the material in front of the blade. A variety of tooth forms are used for this type of band.

Refer to Tooth Form and Set on pages 38 to 41 for information on tooth forms.

2-14. *In friction-sawing, a high blade speed is used to produce heat. This softens the metal and makes it easier to remove with the saw teeth.*

FOUNDRY BAND

A foundry blade is very thick, usually about .050 inch, so it must be used on band saws with at least 36-inch-long blades. This blade has an extremely heavy set that discourages binding or pinching. It is used to cut waste off metal castings. It usually has a pitch of 3 TPI, and a raker set of hook teeth.

SANDING BAND

A sanding band is often provided as an accessory with consumer-grade band saws. It is used to smooth the wood. There is usually a platen to hold the sandpaper in place (2-15).

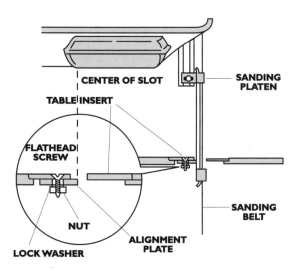

2-15. A sandpaper belt, used to smooth wood, is provided as an accessory with consumer-grade band saws. A platen is used to support the sanding belt.

POLISHING BAND

A polishing band, as its name suggests, is used to polish objects. There is usually a platen that holds the band in place.

FILE BAND

The file band is an industrial band. Short pieces of file are attached to a flexible band (2-16). Dif-

ferent types of file bands are available. A platen similar to the platen for a sanding band is used to support the file band to prevent it from deflecting as pressure is applied to it.

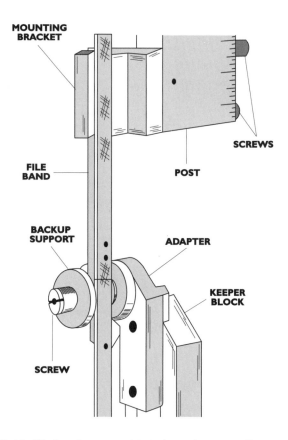

2-16. File bands are used in industrial settings. Short pieces of file are attached to a flexible band.

ROUND BAND

Round bands are used on specially designed band saws. There are two types of round bands. One is a spiral band (2-17). The other is a round grit band. Both are made by DoAll. The grit used is either made of aluminum oxide, diamond, or Borazon. This allows cutting from all directions, not just the front of the blade. This is particularly useful when using CNN (computer-controlled) equipment to guide the material.

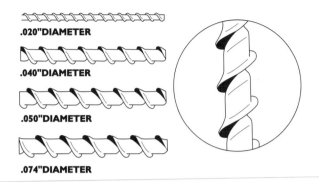

.020"DIAMETER

.040"DIAMETER

.050"DIAMETER

.074"DIAMETER

2-17. Spiral bands are round bands used on specially designed band saws that can cut from any direction.

KNIFE BAND

The knife band doesn't have teeth. Like a knife, it has a straight blade, a scallop, or a wavy edge. Knife bands give a clean cut without sawdust or waste.

Knife bands are used on a number of materials, including the following:

Cardboard	Insulation
Cloth	Metals
Cork	Paper
Coils	Plastics
Foam Rubber	Rubber
Frozen Food	Sponge

The straight knife band is perhaps the most useful of the knife bands. It can be used to cut cardboard, foam, and plastic mesh.

Choosing the Length of Blade

Another factor is choosing band-saw blades is to make sure that the correct length of blade is being used for the band saw. Band-saw blades are sold either in a single-blade length or in rolls of 100, 250, and 500 feet. If the band saw has a brazer or welder, it is more economical to purchase blades by the coil.

The length of blade needed for the band saw may be found in the owner's manual, stamped on the band saw, or stamped on the box the previous blade came it. If it isn't, or if the band-saw user wants to double-check its length, it can be calculated from the following formula: $L = 3.14X + 2 + Y$. In this formula, L represents the length (in inches) of the band-saw blade. X represents the diameter (in inches) of either the upper or lower wheel. Y is the distance (in inches) between the wheel centerlines.

Before the length of the band saw is measured, the upper (tension) wheel should be adjusted so that it is located between the fully up and fully down positions. This midpoint will allow adjustment if the blade is made slightly long or short.

Another way of determining a blade's length is to take a flexible tape measure and wrap it around both wheels.

Testing the Blade

The only way to be sure that the correct blade has been chosen is to test it. Check the quality of the cut on a piece of scrap that is the same species of wood and the same size as your project (2-18).

If dissatisfied with the quality of the cut, make sure that the blade has been correctly tensioned before considering its cutting characteristics. (See Tensioning a Blade on pages 46 to 51 for more information.) A well-tensioned blade will often change. As it heats up from use, it will expand. As it expands in length, it decreases in tension.

When thick material is being sawn for long periods of time—especially when thick and dense wood such as hard maple is being cut—the blade may have to be retensioned to compensate for this expansion. If tension is increased to maintain blade performance, it is important that

2-18. *Testing a blade on a piece of scrap is the best way to make sure that the correct blade is being used.*

the tension is released and the blade allowed to cool and, consequently, decrease to its original length. If the tension is not released, the blade will be overtensioned by the time it cools down.

Ordering Blades

Blades can be bought locally at hardware dealers or through mail-order woodworking catalogues. Some hardware dealers and sharpening shops sell blade stock and will make a blade to the required length. However, this may take time, and it may be prudent to call them ahead of time.

Tensioning a Blade

TENSIONING PRINCIPLES

Blade tension keeps the blade straight. The blade is stretched taut between the wheels. The tension is applied when the adjustable wheel is moved away from the other wheel. The greater the weight (tension), the greater the resistance to side pressure or blade deflection.

One of the most important factors affecting band-saw performance—and the easiest one to change—is the tension of the blade. Blade tension keeps the blade straight between the wheels. It also keeps the blade stiff so that it doesn't flex or deflect during the cut. A poor-quality saw that is well-tensioned will perform better than a quality band saw that is poorly tensioned.

Here is how blade tensioning works: Wheels on the band saw suspend the blade. The top wheel rotates freely. The bottom wheel rotates under power and drives the blade. The top wheel is adjustable up and down by means of a threaded rod. Moving the top wheel upward tightens the blade and increases blade tension. The threaded rod compresses a spring as the tension is increased. That spring is a shock absorber.

The tension on each side of the blade is roughly even. When the blade starts to cut, the blade tension changes. The blade is pulled through the wood by the bottom wheel rotation. The act of cutting creates a dragging effect on the blade. During the sawing process, the tension becomes greatest between the bottom wheel and the workpiece (2-19). The harder and thicker the workpiece or the faster the material is fed into the work, the greater the dragging effect, and the greater the tension between the bottom wheel and the workpiece.

It is important to have enough tension on the blade so that it is fairly equal above and below the table. If the tension on both sides of the workpiece is not equal, the blade will be harder to control. Decreasing the feed rate decreases the drag on the blade, thus lessening the need for tension.

If the band-saw blade doesn't have enough tension, it will flex during the cut (especially a

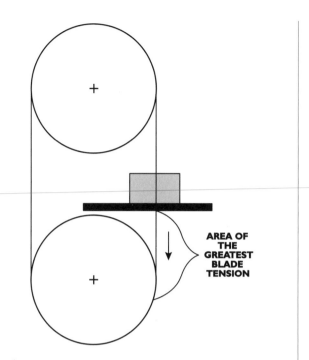

2-19. *As the band saw cuts, the workpiece produces a dragging effect on the blade. This dragging effect increases the tension between the workpiece and the bottom wheel.*

barrel cut) until it tensions itself. The blade will follow the path of least resistance and deflect at the point of greatest stress, which is the saw cut. As the blade deflects, the tension on the blade increases until it reaches a more appropriate tension. This means that the band-saw blade literally tensions itself.

This self-tensioning phenomenon is evident in experiments. A slightly undertensioned blade will make a slightly barreled cut. (Barrel cuts are discussed in the next section.) A grossly undertensioned blade will make an extremely barreled cut. If the band-saw user stops the saw before the very end of a barrel cut and checks the blade tension, it will be close to the proper amount of tension.

It is essential that there is enough tension on the blade to prevent it from flexing during the cut. Once the blade starts to flex, it is very diffi-

cult, if not impossible, to reverse it. The blade follows its wayward path. But how much tension is needed? It has to be enough to equalize the tension on the blade both above and below the table. Simply put, it should be enough to keep the blade straight on each side of the workpiece.

Indications of a Poorly Tensioned Blade

When the blade is not correctly tensioned, noticeable problems will occur when it cuts. The first thing that will be noticed is a condition generally known as a wandering cut. If a blade isn't sufficiently tensioned, it will flex as it cuts. The cut on thin wood (less than one inch thick) won't stay straight and will be hard to control (2-20). This is more of a problem when the intention is to cut straight.

Another condition called blade lead occurs when a blade pulls to one side. Blade lead can be caused by a number of things other than insufficient tension, including poor wheel alignment, poor tracking, uneven teeth, or uneven sharpening.

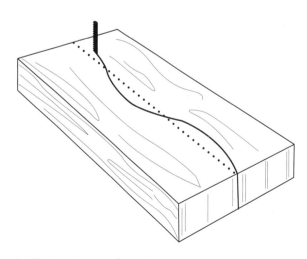

2-20. *If a blade isn't sufficiently tensioned, it won't stay straight on thick wood. The result will be a "wandering" cut.*

When curves are being cut, it isn't difficult to compensate for a wandering blade or blade lead.

When thicker stock is cut with an undertensioned blade, another phenomenon called a barrel cut occurs (2-21). The blade will flex sideways in the work, making a curved cut. This is very frustrating and wasteful. During the cut, the blade will maintain a fairly straight course, progressively straying from the desired line. As the cut progresses, the band-saw user will feel the blade pulling the wood to one side, which indicates that something is wrong with the cut. If this happens, the fingers should not be on the side of the workpiece nearest the blade! The blade can flex enough to come out of the side of the board.

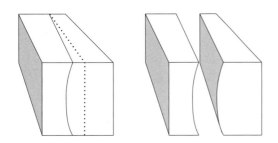

2-21. An insufficiently tensioned blade can also cause a "barrel" cut in thick stock. A barrel cut will be curved from top to bottom and crooked from front to back.

When a barrel cut has been made, two things are noticeable. First, the cut will not be straight from front to back. Secondly, the final cut will curve through the thickness of the workpiece from the top to bottom. By the end of the cut, the blade will be very hot because it has flexed enough to rub hard against the guides, causing friction and heat. This can all contribute to blade breakage.

If wandering or barrel cuts are being made, how does the band-saw user know for sure that a lack of blade tension is causing them? One way to determine is to increase the tension. If this doesn't work, there may be one or more other factors responsible. These factors include the following:

1. Dull blade. (See Determining and Preserving Blade Life on pages 53 to 59 to determine if a blade is dull and ways to preserve blades.)

2. Poorly set guides and/or thrust bearings. (See pages 30 and 31 for more information.)

3. Poor wheel alignment and tracking. (See Chapter 3 for more information.)

5. Not enough of a tooth set. This will give the same slow, labored cut as a dull blade.

6. Uneven set or sharpening. This will cause the blade to "lead," which means that the blade will cut faster on one side and pull in that direction.

7. Blade speed too slow. Correct this by feeding the material more slowly or increasing the blade speed.

8. Proper operator technique. If this is the case, experiment with different feed speeds. A slower feed will often improve the blade's cutting performance because it requires less tension.

These problems can be corrected by readjusting the band saw (refer to pages 67 to 82 for more information on this), changing operating technique, or by changing the blade. Try only one change at a time.

Tensioning Procedures and Guidelines

Tensioning the blade consists of adjusting the upper wheel assembly up or down by turning the knob or hand wheel while measuring the tension on the blade (2-22). Because the upper wheel assembly is adjustable, it allows for slight variations in blade length.

It is important that constant tension be applied to the blade and that there is something to absorb the shock generated by this tension. On newer saws, a spring is used for this. On older saws, a

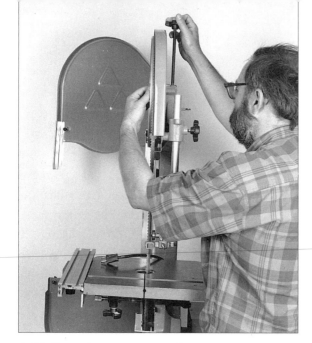

2-22. *To apply tension to the blade, adjust the upper wheel assembly upward by turning the knob or hand wheel while simultaneously measuring the tension on the blade.*

weight is used. After the blade becomes tight, further tension compresses the spring. This spring applies a constant tension to the blade, which is important if the saw has eccentric wheels, that is, wheels that are not perfectly round.

The correct amount of tension is essential for efficient sawing. Ideally, there should be enough tension to ensure a good cut, but not so much that the saw or blade is damaged. Consideration must be given to the whole range of factors, including the type of blade being used, the feed rate, and the thickness and hardness of the material being cut. For example, more tension is needed when wide blades are being used, hard, thick stock is being cut, or material is being cut with a dull blade and at a fast feed rate.

Measuring Tension

There are several methods for measuring tension, but no foolproof technique. With experience, the band-saw user will learn how much tension is required for a particular situation. Following are several methods.

Tension Scales

Most machines have a tension scale (2-23 and 2-24). Tension scales are designed to indicate the compression of the spring. Generally, the greater the spring compression, the greater the blade tension.

2-23. *The tension gauge on this Sears band saw is an arm (visible to the left of the top wheel) that swings upward as the blade tension is increased.*

2-24. *The spring on this 14-inch Delta band saw can be seen through a slot in the casting. The scale indicates the compression of the spring as the blade tension is increased. The larger the blade, the greater the spring compression required to tension it.*

Tension scales don't register the tension of the blade until the blade is relatively taut, so variations in blade length do not make any difference. They are adequate for work that is less than two inches thick.

Over a period of time, the spring will lose its stiffness, particularly if it is under constant tension. This is one of the reasons why the tension should not be released when the saw is not being used. If the spring loses its stiffness, the scale will be off. To adequately tension a blade, a higher setting may have to be used. For example, a ¼-inch blade will have to be adjusted to a ⅜-inch setting on the scale to ensure adequate tension.

Strain Gauges

The section Tension Scales describes how to measure blade tension using a tension scale. Most band saws are fitted with tension scales. However, these scales give only a rough approximation of the proper tension. Strain gauges are more accurate blade-tension indicators that clamp at different positions on the blade. These gauges measure the tension between two fixed points on the blade. Tension on these gauges is measured in pounds per square inch (PSI). Strain gauges are more appropriate for metal sawing, where high tension is commonly used.

PROBLEMS ASSOCIATED WITH OVERTENSIONING

Although having enough tension on the blade is important, there should not be an excessive amount. Following are problems associated with overtensioning:

1. If the blade is very tight, the spring will compress completely. When this happens, the spring no longer functions as a shock absorber and cannot cushion the blade and the band saw from sudden shock—especially if the wheels are eccentric, that is, are not perfectly round.

2. The band-saw shaft can be damaged. The band-saw wheel is designed to withstand a certain force. This tolerance level is more than enough for a normally tensioned blade—that is, a blade tensioned according to the saw's scale. When a blade is tensioned at this level, the shaft will last forever. However, when the blade is overtensioned and the metal on the band-saw shaft is stressed beyond a certain limit, the shaft will eventually fail.

3. Metal fatigue will happen more easily. The revolving blade is the one place on the band saw where the flexing cycles that cause metal fatigue are inadvertently applied. The greater the excessive force, the fewer the number of cycles it takes to cause the failure. Therefore, it is important that too much tension is not applied for too long a period of time.

4. The band saw may become misaligned. A saw that is well-aligned at normal tension can be pulled out of alignment as the tension is increased.

Adequate tension is important for good band-saw performance. However, it is equally important that the correct blade is used, that it has been tracked properly, and that the wheels are correctly aligned. There is a problem with the band saw if the operator has to greatly exceed the tension-scale setting on the saw to get an acceptable performance from the blade. If this problem is not corrected and the operator continues to use excessive tension, there is a chance that the band saw will be damaged.

Strain gauges, which are expensive, are listed in the catalogues of some blade manufacturers. Because these devices are expensive, they are impractical for the small-shop user. It is, therefore, important for the individual craftsperson to be able to determine blade tension through other, less expensive means, as described below.

Measuring and Adjusting Tension by Sound

The easiest way to measure and adjust blade tension is to use sound. Slowly increase the tension while plucking the back of the blade (opposite the teeth). To pluck the blade, hook a finger over it, pull it sideways, and then let it go. A musical note like the one created by a guitar string will be heard. Pluck the blade on its coasting side opposite the blade guides. The narrower the blade, the higher the sound should be. Conversely, the wider the blade, the more bass-like the sound should be.

The sound is caused by the blade vibrating under tension. As the tension is increased, the sound becomes less flat and more clear. This indicates that the blade is in the process of being properly tensioned. When a blade is overtensioned, the sound will decrease because the blade will vibrate less. With a little practice, this can become an easy way to check blade tension. Try for the clearest musical sound.

Measuring and Adjusting Tension by Blade Deflection

Some band-saw users determine blade tension by how much the blade deflects when side pressure is applied to it. To use this technique, raise the top guide assembly all the way up. This will expose at least six inches of blade. Then push on the side of the blade with moderate force (2-25). The more tension used, the stiffer the blade. The stiffer the blade, the less the amount of deflec-

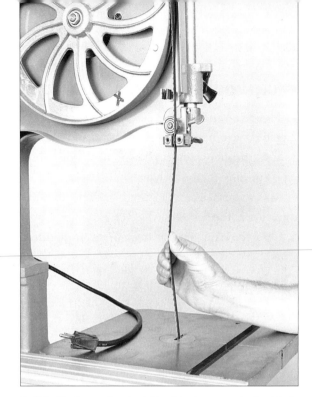

2-25. *Blade tension is defined by how much the blade deflects when side pressure is applied to it.*

tion. With moderate force, the blade should flex about ¼ inch. "Moderate force" is different for each person. The actual deflection of ¼ inch isn't the indicator; it is how much force it takes to deflect it that far.

Measuring blade tension by how much it deflects is a method that, like the use of sound, can be developed with practice.

Folding and Storing Blades

After a blade is used, it should be folded and stored. Wear gloves and eye protection when doing this. There are several different techniques for folding a blade. 2-26 and 2-27 show two primary techniques. Most people prefer the technique shown in 2-26 because they can use both their hands and one foot to hold the blade.

The folding instructions for both techniques are on the following page.

TECHNIQUE NUMBER ONE (2-26):

1. Hold one end of the blade with a foot.

2. Hold the other end with one hand and twist it.

3. Use the free hand to hold the blade while repositioning the other hand.

4. Make another twist of the blade in the same direction as the first twist. This creates three loops.

5. Open the hand so that all of the loops are captured.

TECHNIQUE NUMBER TWO (2-27):

1. Hold the blade so that the thumbs are pointed in opposite directions.

2. To twist the blade, rotate hands in opposite directions. Two loops are created.

3. Twist the blade again. The additional twist has created a third loop. The blade is now ready for storage.

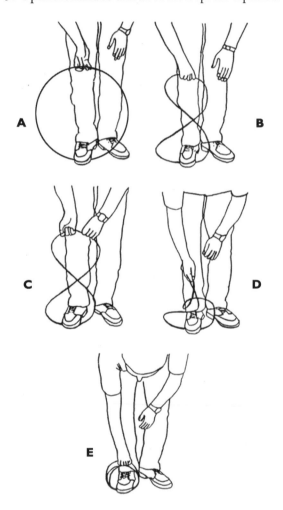

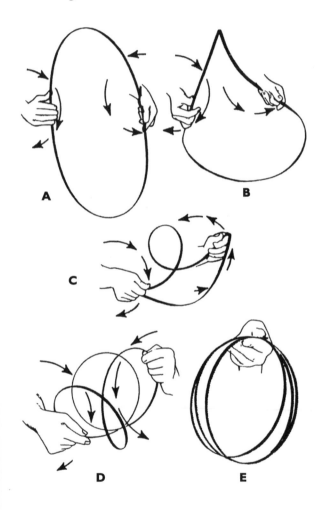

2-26. *This technique for folding a blade is the more popular one because band-saw users can use both their hands and one foot to hold the blade. A: A foot is used to hold one end of the blade. B: The other end of the blade is held with one hand and then twisted. C: The blade is held with the free hand while the other hand is repositioned on the blade. D: The blade is twisted again in the same direction as the first twist; this creates three loops. E: The hand is opened so that all of the loops are captured.*

2-27. *A second technique for folding a blade. A: The blade is held so that the thumbs are pointed in opposite directions. B and C: The hands are rotated in opposite directions. This twists the blades and creates two loops. D and E: The blade is twisted again. The additional twist creates a third loop.*

UNFOLDING BLADES

Be careful when unfolding a blade—especially when using wide blades, because they have a lot of spring. Wear gloves and use eye protection. Always hold the blade away from you. Never try to catch it or to control it with your body. Hold one loop with one hand, and let the blade recoil at arm's length. Always turn your face away from an uncoiling blade.

After the blade has been unfolded, it should be inspected. Try to avoid using blades with cracks, bends, or kinks.

STORAGE TECHNIQUES

String or wire can be used to hold the blade in its folded position. Pipe cleaners work very well and are reusable. Be careful when folding a blade to store it. Many woodworkers accidentally break blades because they put too much pressure on the blade's weld.

Determining and Preserving Blade Life

There are two areas on a blade to be concerned with when determining whether the blade is still usable: its body and the tip of the tooth. These are the two parts that suffer the most from wear. When the tip becomes dull or the blade breaks, the usable life of the blade is over. It is possible to weld the broken blade or sharpen its tooth tip to extend its usable life. (See Welding Blades on pages 59 to 61 for more information.) However, this is usually not cost-effective except in production settings.

Ideally, band-saw teeth should be close to the end of their usable life cycles when the blade body breaks. The body should not break when the teeth are still sharp.

The blade body has to be flexible to withstand the constant flexing/straightening cycle. If it is too hard, it will be brittle and break too easily. The teeth, on the other hand, have to be hard. The harder they are, the more resistant they are to wear and heat. Heat is produced by cutting. The harder and thicker the material, the more heat that is produced. Extreme heat is destructive to the tooth tip, decreasing its ability to stay sharp and resist wear. When metal is being cut, a coolant is often used to help dissipate heat buildup.

Destructive heat buildup is not usually a problem with a band saw unless it runs for a long time. Small blades such as ⅛-inch- or 1/16-inch-wide blades suffer more from heat buildup because they don't dissipate heat as well as larger blades. The large blade body can absorb heat from the tooth.

Blade hardness is important because in contemporary woodworking the tendency today is to simply disgard the blade rather than sharpen or refile it. In the past, woodworking factories usually had a person who filed blades full-time. Today, it is difficult, if not impossible, to find someone who will still sharpen band-saw blades because blades are now relatively inexpensive in relationship to labor.

Refer to Blade-Hardness Characteristics and Metal Composition, which follows. It discusses the hardness characteristics of four groups of blades comprised of different metals.

BLADE-HARDNESS CHARACTERISTICS AND METAL COMPOSITION

Band-saw blades can be broken down into four groups according to their metal composition and their hardness. These groups are spring-steel blades, flex-back carbon blades, hard-back carbon blades, and bi-metal blades. Each is discussed on the following pages.

Spring-Steel Blades

Originally, all band-saw blades were made of spring steel. Spring-steel blades are still popular. They are usually silver in color. The teeth and body of spring-steel blades measure at Rc 36-42. This is not particularly hard. However, the blade is soft enough to be flexible, so it will not break. It is hard enough to be used on soft wood, but dulls fairly quickly on hard wood, especially thick, hard wood.

Spring-steel blades illustrate the problems common with many tools: how to make them hard without sacrificing their toughness. If the metal is too hard, it becomes brittle. This is especially true of the blade body because of its flexing cycle. Therefore, the bodies of some spring-steel blades are not hardened, to keep them flexible, while the teeth are hardened (2-28). Harder teeth stay sharp longer.

There are a number of techniques for hardening the teeth. The tip can be induction-hardened with an electrical current or "flame"-hardened with heat. First the teeth are cut in the soft body, and then they are finish-ground and set. The last stage is the hardening process.

Spring-steel blades are suitable for cutting soft woods.

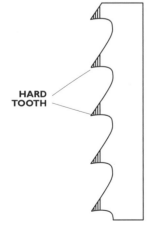

HARD TOOTH

2-28. The teeth on some spring-steel blades are hardened. This makes them last longer, which is essential when they are used to cut hard wood. The bodies of spring-steel blades are not hardened, so they remain flexible.

ABOUT THE ROCKWELL HARDNESS SCALE

The Rockwell Hardness Scale is a means of measuring material hardness. The hardness of the material is determined by measuring its resistance to indentation. Metals are measured on the Rockwell Subgroup C scale (usually abbreviated Rc), so this is the means used to indicate the hardness of band-saw blades.

The higher the number on the Rockwell Hardness Scale, the harder the material. A tooth measuring one point greater than another tooth on the Rockwell Hardness Scale is 100 percent more abrasion-resistant, or durable. In the section Blade-Hardness Characteristics and Metal Composition there are references to the hardness of band-saw blades based on the Rockwell C Scale.

Carbon Blades

Spring-steel blades have limited abrasion resistance and red-heat hardness, that is, durability and the ability to withstand heat in the cutting operation. Carbon blades, which are black, have more carbon content than spring-steel blades, so their teeth are much harder. They are practical to use in metal-cutting.

The teeth on carbon blades are hard. They measure 64 on the Rockwell C Scale (2-29). This is about the hardness of a good chisel. When the teeth are hardened this much, their resistance to wear and red-hot hardness is greatly increased.

The teeth on carbon blades can withstand heat of up to 400 degrees Fahrenheit. This is important when cutting metal because high temperatures are generated. It is less important when cutting wood unless the blade is used in constant day-long production or to cut exotic woods, which are usually rather hard and have minerals that are very abrasive.

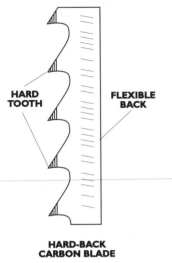

HARD TOOTH **FLEXIBLE BACK**

HARD-BACK CARBON BLADE

2-29. The teeth on carbon blades are hard, measuring 64 on the Rockwell C Scale. Carbon blades have either flexible or hard backs. Flexible backs are softer, measuring Rc 28-34. This softer back extends the flex life of the saw because the blade can withstand repeated flexing around the wheels of the band saw without breaking.

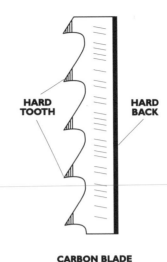

HARD TOOTH **HARD BACK**

CARBON BLADE

2-30. Hard-back carbon blades are used to cut metal. The back of the blade is hardened to Rc 43-47. The hard back prevents the premature wear that can occur on the back of the blade because of the heavy feed pressure common in metal-sawing.

There are two types of carbon blades: flexible- and hard-back blades. Each is discussed below.

Flexible-Back Carbon Blade

The back of a flexible or "flex-back" carbon blade, which measures 28-34 on the Rockwell C Scale, is soft and more flexible than the back of a spring-steel blade. Its teeth are hard and durable, and the blade's body is soft enough but not too brittle.

Flexible-back carbon blades are usually used for woodworking and for cutting soft metals.

Hard-Back Carbon Blades

The back of a hard-back carbon blade has a hardness of Rc 43-47 (2-30). This is important when cutting metal. The increased hardness increases the tensile strength of the blade, which allows the blade to tolerate the high tension used for metal-cutting. The hard back increases its beam strength, which helps the blade resist deflection under the heavy sawing pressure (feed pressure) that is used in a production metal-cutting situation. It also prevents "mushrooming" at the back of the blade that occurs if the back is too soft. This "mushrooming" is also called cold-

forming. If a blade is going to be resharpened, its ability to resist cold-forming is especially important.

The hard back prevents "work-hardening," in which the back of the blade becomes brittle and starts to crack. If a blade starts to crack or break from the back, it usually means that too much feed pressure is being used.

A hard-back blade does not stretch as much as other blades when it gets warm. It works best on a large saw with large wheels. The hard back decreases the blade's flex life. Because of the additional heat-training, a hard-back carbon blade is more expensive, which means that it is more suited to a commercial or professional setting.

A hard-back blade isn't especially important for woodworking, and is not worth the extra expense. A "flex"-back blade is sufficient unless hard, exotic woods are being cut.

Bi-Metal Blades

The bi-metal blade (2-31) was developed to cut various types and shapes of metal. The blade looks like a carbon blade, but is usually a uniform medium-gray color. Like the carbon blade, it has hard teeth and a softer body. A piece of cobalt

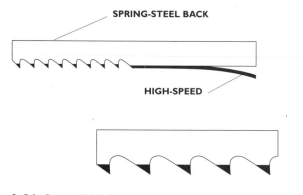

2-31. *Bi-metal blades are made by laminating a high-speed-steel strip to a spring-steel back. Then the teeth are ground. They were developed to cut various types of metal.*

(high-speed) steel laminated to the body forms the teeth (2-32 and 2-33). The back is usually measured at Rc 47-51, and the tips at Rc 66-69. A blade this hard is useful for extremely hot temperatures of up to 1100 degrees Fahrenheit. In comparison, a band-saw blade used on wood cuts at temperatures that rarely reach 300 degrees Fahrenheit.

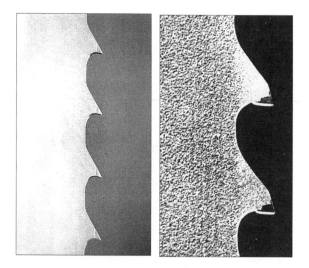

2-32 *(above left).* A close-up of a bi-metal blade with high-speed-steel hook teeth. 2-33 *(above right).* Carbide teeth are individually welded to the body of the bi-metal blade.

Bi-metal blades can withstand much higher tension than carbon blades. In fact, the blade can tolerate the maximum tension that can be generated with a consumer-grade band saw. The high tension increases beam strength. This is useful in metal-cutting because so much feed pressure is used.

Bi-metal blades are designed to be used at 400 feet per minute to ensure maximum blade life. A wood-cutting band saw runs at about seven times that speed, or approximately 2800 feet per minute.

There are several disadvantages to using a bi-metal blade. Because the bi-metal blade is able to tolerate high tensions, the operator may not be privy to the warning signs that indicate that an overtensioned blade may break. As a result, he can actually overtension the bi-metal blade so that it exceeds the safety threshold on a consumer band saw, and consequently, temporarily or permanently twist the frame. Excessive tension can also ruin or damage the wheels and break the shafts.

Another problem that occurs when a bi-metal blade is used to cut wood on a band saw is a phenomenon called harmonic vibration. Most blades vibrate under certain situations. This vibration is often caused by a combination of factors such as blade speed, tension, feed pressure, and the workpiece material being cut. Harmonic vibration roughens the cut and slows the cutting process. If it continues for a long time, it shortens blade life. It can cause the teeth to greatly outlast the body.

The bi-metal blade is quite stiff and hard, so more tension has to be applied to the blade to curtail its tendency to vibrate. Also, the bi-metal blade isn't as sharp as a carbon blade because a sharp edge isn't recommended for metal-cutting, so this may add to its tendency to vibrate.

Another disadvantage to using bi-metal blades

is that the woodworking industry has not found them to be cost-effective. Local saw-sharpening shops that rely on repeat business often don't recommend them for woodworking because they have had too much negative feedback from woodworkers who have tried them. Also, bi-metal blades cost three to four times as much as the average carbon blade.

There is one type of bi-metal blade that has been acclaimed by some blade manufacturers and vendors as the ideal blade. This is the high-speed-steel bi-metal blade. However, this blade also has its drawbacks. It fatigues if it is run too fast. This causes the body to break, which, at the speeds used for woodworking, can be dangerous. The lack of fatigue resistance leads to problems when this blade is used with small wheels. The best-sized wheels to use for any bi-metal blades should be at least 18 inches in diameter.

The bi-metal blade may be most applicable in situations that require abrasion resistance, such as when cutting plywood, particleboard, fiberglass, and exotic woods, which have a high mineral content. If a lot of hard woods such as oak or hard maple are being cut, and a saw with wheels at least 14 inches in diameter is being used, a ½-inch, 3 TPI hook bi-blade is a good blade to use.

PRESERVING BLADE LIFE

Band-saw blades are fragile, and require care both on and off the band saw. If the blade is properly cared for, it will last longer and give a better performance. Follow these guidelines to ensure the best possible use out of band-saw blades:

1. Make sure the band saw is in good condition. If the band saw vibrates or has eccentric wheels, wheels that are out of round, the blade's life will be shortened. Vibration is often decreased by good pulley and belt alignment. High-quality cast-iron pulleys and belts often greatly improve blade performance, especially on less-expensive saws.

Refer to Repairing Eccentric Wheels on pages 17 to 20 and Machine Troubleshooting Techniques on pages 30 to 32 for more information concerning these factors.

2. Make sure the band saw is properly adjusted. It is very important that the saw is properly aligned and that the guide and thrust bearings are properly tracked and adjusted. Poorly adjusted metal guides can damage the blade teeth. Nonmetal guides such as Cool Blocks prevent tooth damage and prolong blade life by decreasing the heat caused by friction between the blade and the blocks.

Refer to Adjusting and Aligning Procedures on pages 68 to 82 for more information.

3. Make sure that the blade is correctly tensioned. An over- or undertensioned blade can have a shortened life. It is a good idea to decrease the tension after using the saw. This also applies to the wheels and tires. When decreasing the tension, use the same number of turns on the knob each time. This way, when the time arrives to increase tension again, it can be done quickly and accurately.

4. Use the proper cutting technique. Use a smooth, slow movement. A quick turn can cause a kink, which is a sharp bend in the blade. A blade will usually break at the kink. Feeding too quickly can shorten blade life. Forcing a wide blade around a tight curve twists the body of the blade, which often causes the blade to break. Running the saw for periods of time when the saw is not cutting also isn't good for the blade.

5. Make sure the blade is clean. With some woods such as pine and cherry, the residue can build up on the face of the tooth. In fact, cherry residue can actually become baked on the front of the tooth. The net effect is that the blade will cut as if it is dull, when in reality it is only packed with residue. This is especially true with fine-pitched saw blades. This can also be a problem at times with some green wood, which is unseasoned wood direct from the log. To clean coarse-tooth blades, use a stiff bristle or fine wire brush (2-34). To clean fine-pitch blades, soak the blade in a solution first and then clean it with a very fine wire brush. A number of cleaning products such as ammonia solution, oven cleaner, or turpentine work. Wipe the blade dry.

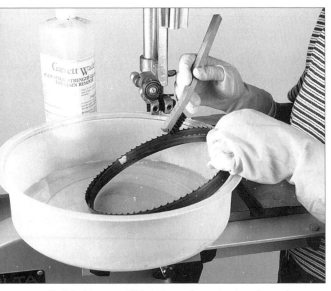

2-34. *Use a stiff bristle or fine wire brush to clean coarse-tooth blades.*

6. Handle the blade with care when it is off the band saw. If storing the blade in a humid place, wipe it with an oil rag. The oil will prevent it from rusting. If a blade has become rusty, wipe it with an oil rag to remove as much rust as is possible. If it is very rusty, steel wool will do a good job of removing the rust.

7. Round the blade back. One way to improve blade performance and extend the life of a blade is to round the back of the blade with a sharpening stone. A round blade back creates a smooth interaction between the thrust bearing and the blade. If the blade rotates slightly, there is no sharp blade corner to dig into the thrust bearing.

Another advantage of rounding the blade's back is that the round process smoothes the weld. A blade with a round back makes tight turns better because the round back has smooth interaction with the saw kerf.

To round a blade's back, first adjust the guides. (Refer to Adjusting the Guide Blocks on pages 79 to 82 for more information.) Next, hold the stone against the corner of the blade for about a minute (2-35). Wear safety glasses when rounding the blade. Do the same thing on the opposite corner.

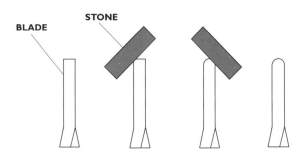

2-35. *To round the back of a blade, first stone the corners. Then slowly rotate the stone around the back. This process takes approximately two or three minutes.*

Next, slowly move the stone to round the back. The more pressure put on the back, the more quickly the metal will be removed. Make sure that the inside of the band saw is free of sawdust, because sparks could start a fire.

One word of caution about rounding the back of a 1/8- or 3/16-inch-wide blade: The pressure on the back of the blade may bring the blade forward off the front of the wheels. To prevent this, it is best to feed wood into the blade during the rounding process. Pass the wood underneath the elevated stone. This keeps the blade in contact with the thrust bearing (2-36).

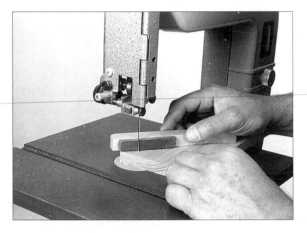

2-36. *Feeding wood into a 1/8- or 1/16-inch-wide blade while rounding it will prevent the stone from pushing the blade forward off the wheels.*

8. Store the blade when you are finished with it. Fold the blade into three loops when storing it. A blade can be hung up in an unfolded position, but it will take up a lot of space on the wall.

Folding a blade into three loops is not difficult if one of the two basic techniques is learned. The principle is the same for both techniques: hold the blade and make one twist, and then make another twist. This creates three loops.

When unfolding a blade, band-saw users should be very careful—especially when using wide blades, which have a lot of spring. Gloves and eye protection should be worn. The blade should always be held away from the body, and the body should never be used to catch or control it. A loop should be held with one hand, and the blade should be allowed to recoil at arm's length. The face should always be turned away from an uncoiling blade. After the blade is unfolded, it should be inspected. Blades with bends, cracks, or kinks should not be used.

Refer to Folding and Storing Blades on pages 51 and 52 for more information.

Welding Blades

Welding is the process of reattaching a broken blade. There are three occasions when the blade is welded: 1, to form the continuous band after the blade is cut to the desired length; 2, after it breaks, to make it usable again (only reweld the blade if it is in good shape); and 3, when it is used to make interior cuts in metal-working. In the third case, the blade is purposely sheared, threaded through a hole, and rewelded. That's why large metal-cutting band saws usually have a welder on their columns (2-37). This makes it easy to shear and reweld the blade quickly without removing the workpiece from the table.

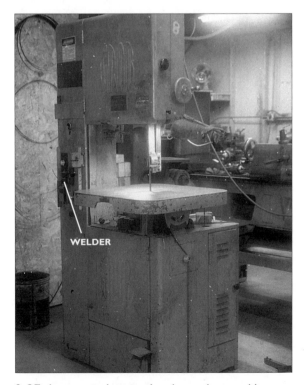

WELDER

2-37. *Large metal-cutting band saws have welders mounted on their columns, to be used when interior cuts are made in metal-working.*

There are two types of blade welding used: Resistance-welding and silver-brazing. Each is discussed below.

RESISTANCE-WELDING

The most commonly used welders used in industrial and professional shops are resistance-type welders (2-38). When using a resistance-type welder, first grind the blade ends square. Then clamp the ends together in the welder and heat them until they fuse together to form a weld. Making a good weld takes skill, care, and practice, and there are a number of things that can go wrong during this process.

2-38. *A close-up of a resistance welder on a metal-cutting band saw. These are the most commonly used welders in industrial and professional shops. They expedite interior-cutting.*

When the band or blade is heated during welding, it is air-hardened and, therefore, is very brittle at the point where it has been welded. Before it can be used, it must be annealed to restore the weld joint to the same hardness and strength as the rest of the band. This is done by reheating it to annealing temperatures and then cooling it slowly. The annealing temperature is detected by the color of the metal. For both carbon and high-speed-steel blades, the proper color is dull cherry-red. Properly annealing the weld is as important as properly making the weld.

After completing the welding and annealing, file or grind the weld smooth (2-39). It is important that both the front and back of the blade are smoothed. A proper weld will be solid and smooth.

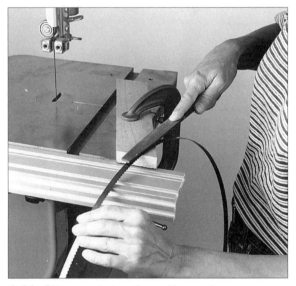

2-39. *Filing or grinding the weld smooth.*

SILVER BRAZING

The alternative to resistance-welding is to braze the joint together using a silver solder alloy between the two blade ends. Properly done, this joint is very strong and flexible. It also can be brazed without the use of expensive or complicated machinery.

To braze the joint together, hold the two blade ends in a vise and flux and heat a small piece of the silver solder alloy with a torch (2-40). This forms the joint.

For a maximum surface area, first hold the blade ends at 20 degrees (2-41). This technique

2-40. *Brazing a blade joint consists of using a propane torch to melt silver solder alloy in the blade. When doing this, hold the two blade ends in a vise.*

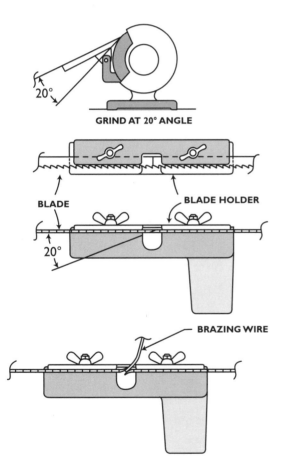

GRIND AT 20° ANGLE

BLADE

BLADE HOLDER

20°

BRAZING WIRE

2-41. *To ensure maximum surface area on the blade, hold the blade ends at 20 degrees.*

takes some practice, but can be mastered and is a good way of salvaging blades that break but still are usable. It is especially useful if a professional resistance welder is not locally available.

There are brazing kits available that can be used to braze a joint together. These kits consist of silver-solder wire, a blade holder, and flux. They are advertised is some mail-order woodworking catalogues.

CORRECTING WELD PROBLEMS

In order for the blade to track and cut properly, the weld must be straight and well-aligned. Many band-saw problems can be traced to an irregularity in the weld. These problems include premature blade breakage, a blade that does not flex properly, a blade that is not welded straight, and problems that occur because the temperature of the welder is not set accurately. Each is discussed below.

Premature Breakage

Experts believe that when a blade breaks, approximately half the time the break should be attributed to the weld, and half the time to the blade body. If it breaks consistently at the weld, the weld is bad. In this case, the blade should be rewelded or returned to the supplier if it breaks in the first 15 minutes of use.

A Blade That is Not Flexible

The blade should be flexible, so that it can withstand a fairly tight bend. Most band-saw users test the weld by flexing it (2-42). If it breaks, it needs to be rewelded. Band-saw users often break a blade when they fold it to store it because they put undue pressure on the weld. The weld should withstand gentle flexing, but it is unreasonable to expect it to make sharp turns.

2-42. *The weld on a blade should be flexible, so that it can withstand a fairly tight bend.*

Blades with Poorly Aligned Welds

The weld on a blade can be aligned with the blade in three possible ways. 2-43 shows these possibilities. The correct weld alignment is shown in A of 2-43. The weld is straight. The alignment shown in C is potentially very destructive because the sharp corner can damage the thrust bearing. When the weld is misaligned as shown in B and C, there will be a distinct ticking sound as the blade runs that is similar to that of a loud clock.

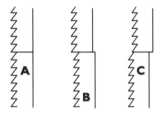

2-43. *Three weld-alignment possibilities on a blade. A shows correct alignment, in which the weld is straight. B and C show a misaligned weld. A weld that is as shown in C will damage the thrust bearing in a short period of time.*

Also make sure that the back of the weld is straight, that is, that it is not longer than the front of the blade. This is not easy to do. During the hardening of the teeth, the front of the blade shrinks. If a blade is resting on its back, it will often rock because the back is convex and the front (tooth) side is concave. Some blades rock worse than others.

Because the blade arches, it is impossible to weld the back of the blade perfectly straight. However, weld it as straight as possible. If it is not straight, the blade will move back and forth on the saw. Sometimes this makes tracking the blade difficult. (See Tracking the Blade on pages 68 to 76 for more information.) It may also be difficult to keep the blade on the saw because it will keep moving forward on the saw. This is because the back of the blade is longer than the front, and unequal pressure is being applied to the wheels.

Incorrect Welder Temperature

To get a good weld, a band-saw user should ensure that the temperature of the welder is set accurately. 2-44 shows a number of problems with the weld caused by an incorrectly set welder. When these occur, the blade should be reground and rewelded.

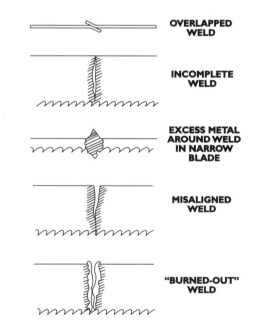

2-44. *If the temperature of the welder is not set correctly, a number of weld alignment problems can occur, as shown here. If the weld has any of these characteristics, reweld it or send it back to the supplier.*

Sharpening Blades

When a blade becomes dull, its ability to cut is compromised. A dull blade should be replaced or resharpened. Because blades are relatively inexpensive today, many woodworkers feel the easiest approach is to replace it. Still, the ability to hand-sharpen a blade is a useful skill, and with practice one can master the technique.

There are two means of sharpening: filing and grinding. Both are discussed in the following sections.

FILING

Filing is the traditional method for sharpening a band-saw blade. There are advantages to filing a blade instead of throwing it away. A properly filed blade is often sharper than a new one and stays sharp for a longer period of time. This is especially true with a fine-pitch blade such as an ⅛-inch, 14 TPI blade. A blade such as a 1/16-inch blade is impractical to sharpen.

Band-saw blades are usually filed by hand, although some saw-sharpening shops use specialized automatic filing machines. A three-corner file is commonly used. A file with a round corner is best.

When filing blades, good light is important, and natural daylight ideal. Hold the blade securely in a vise (2-45). A saw-sharpening vise works best. A metal-working vise can also be used.

When filing, use the same number of strokes on each tooth. Usually three strokes are used. File the teeth straight across, 90 degrees to the body. The teeth should be filed after the teeth are set. The teeth should be set after every three to five sharpenings.

A saw set can be used for setting the teeth. It is best for the person filing the teeth to file those

2-45. Proper blade-filing technique. A good vise and adequate light are essential.

teeth facing him/her first. Then the blade should be reversed and the other teeth filed, with the strokes always away from the filer. This leaves the burr on the inside (2-46). The rakers should be filed in a similar manner to the other teeth, with every other raker filed from the same side.

Some band-saw users like to file the blade on

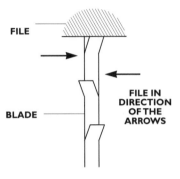

FILING THE BLADE

2-46. *Filing from the inside outward leaves the burr on the inside.*

the saw. To do this, turn the saw blade "inside out" and remount it so that the teeth point up (2-47). Blocks of wood should be clamped together in a vise to prevent the wood from moving while the filing is being done. If a good saw vise is not available, this may be the preferable approach.

Filing is appropriate for softer blades such as spring-steel blades and fine-pitch carbon blades with a standard-tooth form. Harder blades such as hardened spring-steel, carbon, and bi-metal blades should be ground.

GRINDING

The second method of sharpening a band-saw blade is to grind it with a rotating grinding wheel. This is faster than filing, and can remove material that is too hard for a file. If a spacing jig is used, as described in the following section, grinding is a very accurate process.

2-47. *If filing the blade on the saw, turn it "inside-out" and remount it so that its teeth point down.*

2-48 shows a huge automated grinding machine being used to sharpen a band-saw mill blade. The machine automatically coordinates the movement of the blade and the wheel so that the front and back of the blade are sharpened by the stone. 2-49 shows a less-expensive option of sharpening a blade. It consists of using a spacing jig during the grinding process. An adjustable pin is used to stop the movement of the blade, thus spacing each cut. This design is similar to that of a chainsaw filing machine.

2-48. *A 14-inch grinding wheel is being used to sharpen a band-saw-mill blade at Johnson Lumber Company in Charlotte, Michigan. The grinding wheel and the blade movement are coordinated so that the back and the face of the blade are ground.*

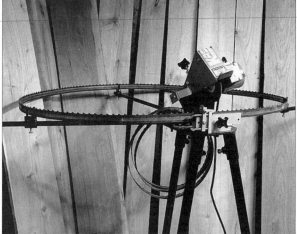

2-49. *A close-up of the Kasco spacing jig and the blade support. The blade shown is 1¼ inches wide.*

BLADE TROUBLESHOOTING TECHNIQUES

The information in this section will help the reader solve problems that occur with band-saw blades. These problems include blade breakage, blades that slow and/or stop, noisy blades, and blades that do not track properly.

Problem	Reason	Solution
1. Blade breakage	Excessively high feed rate	Slow the feed rate
	Poorly adjusted guides or bearings	Readjust guides and bearings
	Blade tension too high	Decrease blade tension. Use only as much as needed to perform an operation. Thick or hard work will require more tension.
	Blade too thick in relationship to wheel diameter and sawing speed	Replace blade

Problem	Reason	Solution
Blade breakage *(continued)*	Poor weld	Replace blade
	Worn tires	Redress or replace tires (pages 21 to 23)
	Dull blade	Blade at end of life cycle and breakage to be expected
	Overheated blade	Blade too fine. Try a coarse blade.
	Improperly adjusted guides or thrust bearings	Readjust guides or thrust bearings
	Poor operator techique	Slow feed rate and avoid twisting blade
2. Noisy blade	Ticking sound as the saw runs caused by poor weld alignment	Stone back and file it round when saw is running. Wear safety glasses for this operation.
	Blade twisted or bent and hits guides	Remove blade and straighten kick, if possible.
	Blade runs quietly and then starts to make ticking sound	Blade has cracked and will break soon. When it does, stop saw and replace blade.
3. Blade will not stay on saw or near middle of wheel	Misaligned wheels	Adjust wheels (pages 67 and 68)
	Too much foreward tilt on top wheel	Line wheels up with straightedge and let blade find its equilibrium on wheels
	Worn tires	If tires are worn, there will be a concavity in middle of tires and blade will not track in the concavity. Re-surface tires so that crown is created again (pages 21 to 23).
	Not enough blade tension	Increase blade tension to recommended amount. Excessive blade tension can cause blade to come off wheels. Relax tension.
4. Blade slows and/ or stops	Blade binds in stock. Keep kerf open.	Do not squeeze workpiece so as to close kerf
	Blades turn in too tight a radius	Select narrower blades
	Blade twists or presses against guides	Use light forward pressure
	Upper blade guide too tight	Readjust upper blade guide
	Oil level low	Check oil level and add oil
	Feed rate too fast	Feed stock more slowly
	V-belt slipping	Increase tension on V-belt
	Pulleys slipping on shafts	Secure pulleys on drive shaft

3 Adjustment and Alignment Procedures

In order for the band saw to operate at its optimum level, it has to be properly tuned and adjusted. This consists of aligning the wheels, tracking and tensioning the blade, adjusting the guide post, squaring the table, and adjusting the thrust bearings and guide blocks. Each of these procedures is discussed in this chapter.

Having a well-tuned and adjusted band saw has many benefits. It makes the work more efficient, more enjoyable, and safer. It also increases cutting options. With a well-tuned band saw, small pieces that are dangerous to cut on table or radial arm saws can be ripped. There is no danger that they will kick back with a band saw. If a well-tuned band saw can help prevent an accident, all the attention given to it is certainly worth the effort.

Aligning Band-Saw Wheels

The first step in aligning the band saw is to check that its wheels are aligned, and, if not, align them. This is a very simple procedure that should only take a few minutes to accomplish, and which should be done as often as needed.

Do the following:

1. *Tension the blade.* Tension the widest blade that can be used on the band saw. Tensioning is the process of stretching the blade taut between the wheels. (Refer to Tensioning a Blade on pages 46 to 51 for more information.) A ½-inch-wide blade is the largest practical blade to use on a consumer band saw. Use the tension scale on the band saw (3-1).

2. *Check that the wheels are parallel to each other.* To do this, put a straightedge in the middle of the wheels with the ½-inch blade tensioned. If it touches the top and bottom of both wheels, the wheels are parallel and aligned with each other, in other words, coplanar (3-2).

If the wheels are not in alignment, the straightedge will not touch the top and bottom of both wheel points (3-3). Instead, it will touch the top and bottom of the top wheel or the top and bottom of the lower wheel. In either case, one of the wheels will have to be moved to make both wheels coplanar.

3. *Measure the misalignment.* If the band-saw user is going to achieve coplanar alignment by adding or removing washers from behind the wheel, it

is important to know how far one of the wheels has to be moved. The way to do this is to measure the misalignment at the top and bottom of the wheel that is not touching the straightedge (3-4). The measurements at both points should be the same. If they are not identical, angle the top wheel until they are. Once they are the same, the amount that the wheel had to be moved is the distance needed to align the wheels (3-5).

4. *Make the adjustment.* On Sears and Inca band saws, the wheels are aligned by using the movable bottom wheels. This is the easiest and most convenient way of aligning the wheels. The bottom wheel is mounted on a shaft in a keyway (a groove on the shaft that prevents the wheel from spinning on the shaft), and the wheel is locked in place with a setscrew. When making the adjustment, loosen the screw and move the wheel the desired amount.

On Delta and Taiwanese band saws, the adjustment is made on the top wheel, which is mounted on a threaded shaft and held secure with a nut. To make the adjustment, unscrew the nut and then remove the wheels. This will expose the washers. Make the alignment by either adding or removing washers. Additional washers can be bought at hardware dealers.

After the first alignment, always rotate the wheels several times to make sure that the blade is tracking properly. Then recheck the alignment.

Tracking the Blade

After aligning band-saw wheels, the next step is to track the blade. Tracking refers to the act of positioning or balancing the band-saw blade on the wheels. Below is information that will help band-saw users track blades properly.

ALIGNING BAND-SAW WHEELS

3-1. The first step in aligning band-saw wheels is tensioning the blade. Tension the widest blade that will be used. Here a 1/2-inch-wide blade is being tensioned on a Sears band saw.

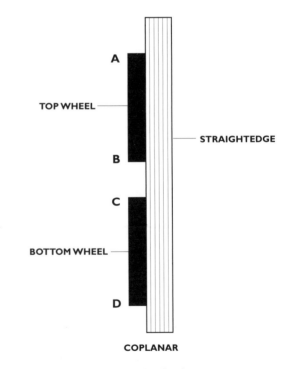

3-2. After tensioning the blade, the next step is to make sure that the wheels are parallel or coplanar to each other. Use a straightedge to do this. The wheels are coplanar if the straightedge touches the tops and bottoms of both wheels. These positions are indicated in the drawings as A, B, C, and D.

ALIGNING BAND-SAW WHEELS (CONTINUED)

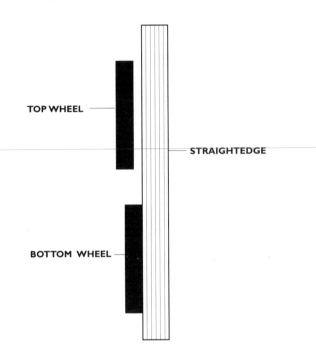

3-3. *If the wheels are not aligned, the straightedge will only touch one wheel point.*

TOP WHEEL

STRAIGHTEDGE

BOTTOM WHEEL

3-4. *With a straightedge against the bottom wheel, use a ruler to measure the distance between the top wheel and the straightedge. The straightedge may have to be held against the bottom wheel with a knee.*

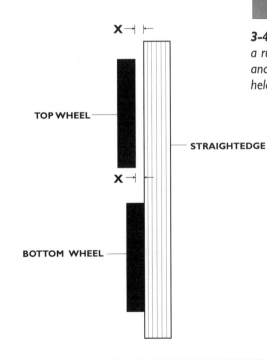

X

TOP WHEEL

STRAIGHTEDGE

X

BOTTOM WHEEL

3-5. *It is important to know how much to move the wheel to make the wheels coplanar. This is X as shown in this drawing. Measure this distance from the top and bottom of the wheel.*

TRACKING PRINCIPLES

There is no external force that holds the blade on the wheels. It remains on the wheels because of two factors: the outside shape of the wheel and the angle of the top wheel.

The *outside shape of the wheel* is determined by the shape of the metal casting on the rim of the wheel. The outside rim of the wheel is covered with a piece of rubber called a tire, which is between ⅛ and ¼ inch thick (3-6). The tire acts as a cushion and a shock absorber. It also prevents the blade from contacting the metal wheel, and thus damaging the teeth.

Wheels either have a flat or a crown shape (3-7). The crown exerts a controlling force on the blade that causes it to ride near the middle, but not exactly in the middle, of the wheel. A flat wheel is designed so that the operator can track the blade either in the middle of the wheel or toward the front of the wheel. Both systems have advantages and disadvantages.

One disadvantage of a crowned wheel is that it provides less surface area between the blade and the tire. This makes it more difficult to track large blades such as a ½ inch-wide blade, which is the best blade to use for straight cuts, especially resawing. Another disadvantage is that if the wheels are not perfectly aligned with each other, the crowns on each wheel will compete for control of the blade. This causes vibration and shortens the life of a blade.

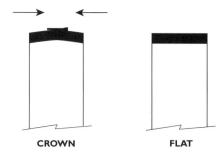

3-7. *Band-saw wheels either have a crown or a flat shape. The crown exerts a controlling force which helps track the blade near the middle of the wheel.*

A flat wheel provides good support for wide blades, but the blade has to be tracked more carefully. With a flat wheel, the blade can be tracked in various positions on the wheel. Wide blades are best tracked toward the front of the tire, often with their teeth off the front wheel. Narrow blades are best tracked toward the middle of the tire.

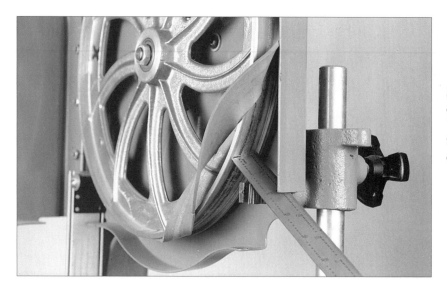

3-6. *The wheel is made of cast metal with a curved rim. The rubber tire is flat and fits tightly over the curved rim, creating the crown.*

The main disadvantage of a flat wheel is that when the tire starts to wear, a depression forms in the tire and makes the blades more difficult to track. This can be alleviated by dressing the tire with sandpaper so that there is a crown of about .020 inch, about the thickness of five pieces of paper. (Refer to Restoring the Tire's Original Shape on pages 21 and 22 for more information.)

As mentioned, the second factor that affects the tracking of a blade is the angle of the top wheel. The angle of the top wheel steers the blade in the direction of the tilt (3-8). The usual approach is to tilt the top wheel, usually rear-

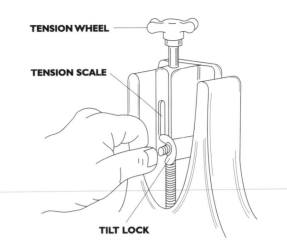

3-9. Tilt the top wheel to track the blade in the middle of the wheel.

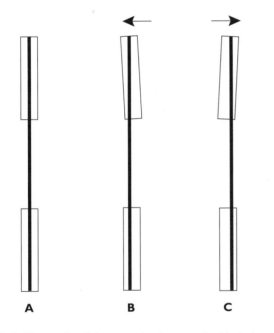

3-8. The angle of the top wheel steers the blade in the direction of the tilt. As shown in A, when the top wheel is centered, the blade is centered. As shown in B and C, when the top wheel tilts to the left and right, the blade tilts in that direction.

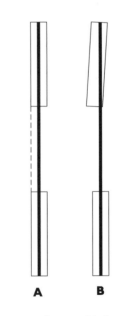

3-10. Use center-tracking on blades that are ³⁄₁₆ inch wide or smaller.

wards, until the blade tracks in the middle of the top wheel (3-9). This approach is the one that is usually recommended in the owner's manual. It is called "center-tracking" (3-10).

Center-tracking works well on blades up to ³⁄₁₆ inch wide. These blades are flexible and the misalignment of the wheel doesn't affect their performance or life expectancy. However, blades wider than ¼ inch are not as flexible as the narrower blades. Track these wider blades with the wheels aligned with each other, rather than with the top wheel angles. This is called "coplanar tracking" because the wheels are in a coplanar position, that is, they lie in the same plane (3-11).

The objective in tracking wide blades is to allow the blade to run as straight as possible. If the wheels are coplanar, the blade will find its own equilibrium and essentially track itself. With coplanar-tracking, the blade exerts the same amount of pressure on the tires at all points of contact. There is no binding, which occurs when the top wheel is angled. The blade will last longer and cut straighter, and will require less tension for good performance.

One of the things noticeable when coplanar-tracking is used is that the blade will have a tendency to track toward the front of the wheels. The reason why this occurs is that the front of the blade is narrower than its back. When the blades are manufactured, their teeth are first ground and then hardened, which causes the front of the blade to shrink in relationship to the back. The difference between the front and the back is greater on wide blades.

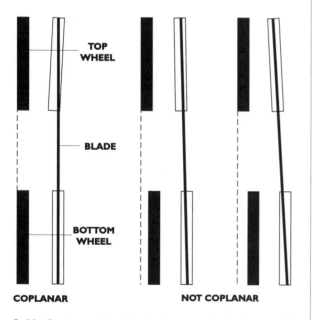

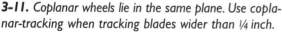

3-11. Coplanar wheels lie in the same plane. Use coplanar-tracking when tracking blades wider than ¼ inch.

TRACKING PROCEDURE

Tracking consists of removing the old blade from the band saw, installing and tensioning the new blade, and then positioning the blade on the wheels using center- or coplanar tracking procedures. Each of these procedures is discussed below. Once the band-saw user has become familiar with these procedures, tracking should only take a minute or two.

Remember to be careful when using blades, especially wide and sharp ones. Some woodworkers prefer to use gloves when handling large blades. Safety glasses are always a must.

Removing the Blade

Many woodworkers do not like to change blades. However, the procedure is not difficult if performed step by step. Here are the steps:

1. Unplug the saw.

2. Remove the mechanism for aligning the table halves (3-12). It will be a pin, a bolt, or a front rail.

3. Unscrew the blade guard or open the hinge (3-13).

4. Remove the throat plate (3-14).

5. Release the blade tension, thus lowering the top wheel (3-15).

6. Expose the wheels by opening or removing the covers.

7. Take the blade off the wheels with both hands and carefully slide it out of the table slot (3-16 and 3-17).

8. Fold the blade (3-18).

Text continues on page 75.

TRACKING PROCEDURES: REMOVING THE BLADE

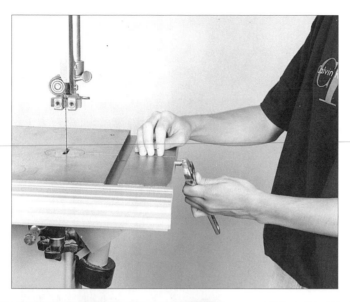

3-12. The steps involved in removing a blade. The first consists of removing the mechanism that aligns the table halves. This can be a pin, bolt, or a front rail.

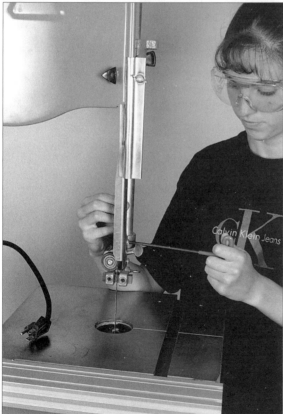

3-13. The blade guard is unscrewed.

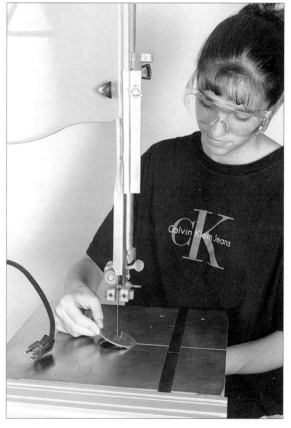

3-14. Next, the throat plate is removed.

TRACKING PROCEDURES: REMOVING THE BLADE (CONTINUED)

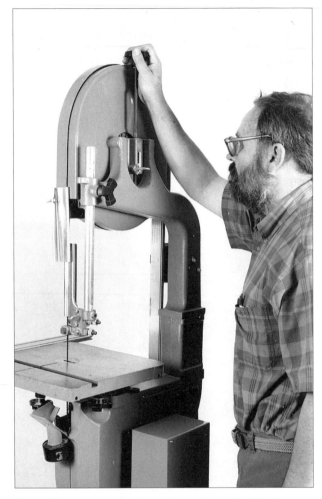

3-15. *The top wheel is lowered to release the blade tension.*

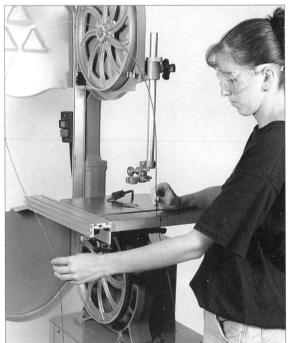

3-16 (right top) and 3-17 (right bottom). *After the covers are opened to expose the wheels, the blade is slid out of the table slot.*

9. Retract the thrust bearings above and below the table (3-19).

10. Loosen the guides on the side of the blade (3-20) and then retract them too. This way, the next blade can be easily installed without any obstructions.

TRACKING PROCEDURES: REMOVING THE BLADE (CONTINUED)

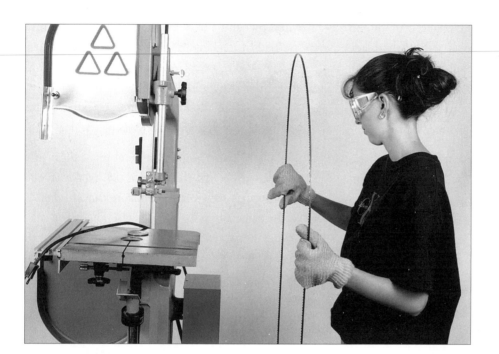

3-18. The blade is folded so it can be stored out of harm's way.

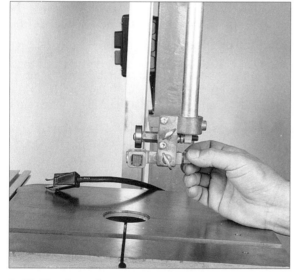

3-19. The thrust bearings are retracted.

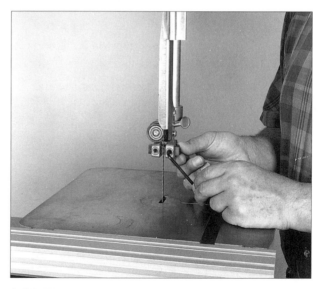

3-20. The guides on the side of the blade are loosened and retracted.

Installing and Tensioning the New Blade

After the old blade has been removed, the next step is to install and tension the new one. Do the following:

1. Uncoil the blade. Remember to use gloves and safety glasses. If it is an unused blade, it may have oil on it. Sometimes manufacturers put oil on blades to prevent rust. Wipe the oil off the blade with a rag or a paper towel. Pull the blade through the rag rearwards so that its teeth don't catch on the rag.

2. Hold the blade up to the saw. Inspect the teeth. If the teeth are pointed in the wrong direction, the blade will have to be turned inside out. To do this, hold the blade with both hands and rotate it.

3. Holding the blade with both hands, with the edges of its teeth facing you, slide it through the table slot and place it on the wheels. Some woodworkers like to handle the blade as it is positioned on the top wheel, because they are then taking advantage of the force of gravity.

4. Position the blade on the area of the wheel where it should be, and then tension it. (Refer to Tensioning a Blade on pages 46 to 51 for more information.) Next, slowly raise the top wheel with the tension knob. Start to rotate the wheels by hand in the normal direction while the blade is still fairly slack. While doing this, notice where the blade is tracking. If it is tracking too far forward or backward on the wheel, make an adjustment with the tilt mechanism.

While rotating the blade with one hand, increase its tension with the other. Continue to do this until the blade has been adequately tensioned. A blade cannot be correctly tracked until the tensioning is completed.

Tracking Methods

After the old blade has been removed and the new one installed and tensioned, the next step is to track the blade. Following are the procedures. Remember, never track the blade with the saw running!

1. When center-tracking the blade, rotate the top wheel by hand and angle the tilt mechanism until the blade is tracking in the middle of the top wheel (3-21). Make several revolutions of the blade to ensure that it stays in the same place on the wheels. Then lock the tilt knob. Center-tracking works best on blades that are up to $\frac{3}{16}$ inch wide.

2. When using coplanar-tracking, align the wheels with a straightedge (3-22). Make several revolutions of the blade to ensure that it remains in the same place on the wheels. The blade may or may not track in the middle of the top wheel. In fact, it will usually track toward the front of the wheels. Tilt the top wheel slightly rearwards if the blade starts to move forward or come off the front of the saw. Then lock the tilt knob. Coplanar-tracking works best with blades that are at least $\frac{1}{4}$ inch wide (3-23).

3. After the blade has been tracked, replace the cover and the blade guard and then plug in the electrical cord. Turn on the saw for a second and then turn it off again. Watch to see how the saw runs. If the blade seems to track well, run it under full power.

Adjusting the Guide Post

After the blade has been tracked, the next step is to adjust the guide post. The guide post is the part of the band saw to which the top guide assembly (consisting of the guides and thrust bearings) is attached (3-24). It is a moveable post

TRACKING METHODS: CENTER- AND COPLANAR-TRACKING

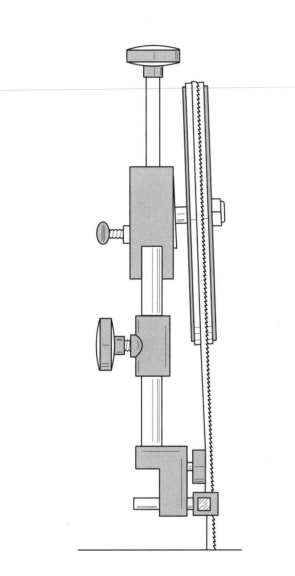

3-21. *In center-tracking, the top wheel is rotated by hand until the blade tracks in the middle of it.*

3-22. *The first step in coplanar-tracking is aligning the wheels with a straightedge.*

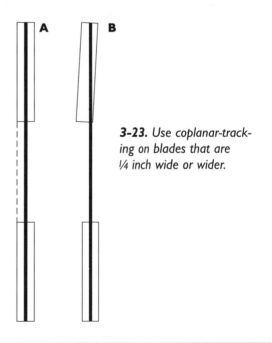

3-23. *Use coplanar-tracking on blades that are ¼ inch wide or wider.*

that is raised or lowered to accommodate different thickness of wood.

The guide post is adjusted before the thrust bearings and the guide blocks. This is because the thrust bearings, which are the mechanisms above and below the band-saw table used to stop the rearward movement of the blade (3-25), must be aligned with each other. If the guide post is not adjusted, that is, if it does not go straight up and down, the bearings will not be aligned.

Adjust the post so that there is about ¼ inch of clearance between the bottom of the post and the top of the workpiece (3-26). The top thrust bearing and the top guide blocks should be checked for alignment each time the post is adjusted.

ADJUSTING THE GUIDE POST

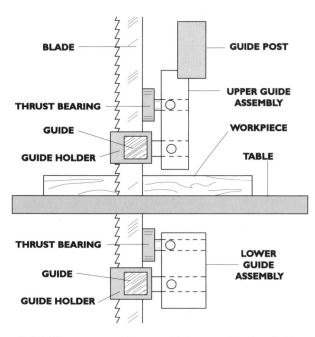

3-24. The upper guide assembly is a casting that holds the bearings and the guide holder.

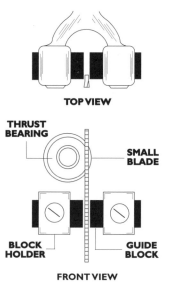

3-25. Thrust bearings are located behind the blade and prevent the blade from being shoved rearward by the workpiece. The guide blocks are located on each side of the blade and prevent the blade from twisting and deflecting.

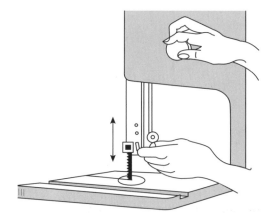

3-26. The guide post is adjustable up and down. The top guide assembly should be positioned above the blade to decrease exposure to the blade and promote safety.

Squaring the Blade and the Table

Before the thrust bearings and the guide blocks can be adjusted, the band-saw user has to ensure that the blade and table are square, or at 90 degrees, to each other. Use a high-quality square for this procedure (3-27). Check the squareness frequently.

3-27. *Use a square to ensure that the blade and table are at 90 degrees to each other.*

Adjusting the Thrust Bearings

The next step is to adjust the thrust bearings. The thrust bearings, as mentioned earlier, are round bearings on the wheel used to stop the rearward movement of the blade. There are usually two thrust bearings, one above and one below the table.

To adjust the thrust bearings, position the blade weld opposite the bearings. Use the blade as a straightedge, remembering that the weld is the least-straight part of the blade.

For blades 3/16 inch wide or wider, the two thrust bearings should be positioned about 1/64 inch behind the blade (3-28). When the cut begins, the blade moves rearwards and contacts the thrust bearings. (The thrust bearings should never contact the blade when the saw is not cutting except on narrower blades such as the 1/8- and 1/4- inch blades.) When the cutting stops, the blade should move forward again, and the bearings should stop rotating.

A feeler gauge or a dollar bill folded twice can be used to determine the correct space between the blade and the bearings. For narrower blades such as the 1/8- and 1/16-inch blades, the bearing should contact the back of the blade. The 1/16-inch blade should be supported with the bearing moved forward about 1/64 inch to give it extra support.

Adjusting the Guide Blocks

The next step is adjusting the guide blocks. The four guide blocks are held in place by guide holders that are paired with each thrust bearing above and below the table. Some band saws have bearings instead of solid metal guides.

Place the metal guide blocks about .004 inch away from the blade. This is the thickness of a

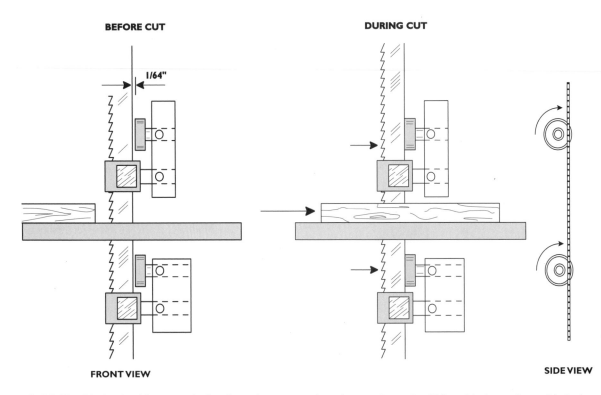

BEFORE CUT

1/64"

FRONT VIEW

DURING CUT

SIDE VIEW

3-28. *The blade should not touch the thrust bearings unless the saw is cutting. When blades at least 3/16 inch wide are being used, the two thrust bearings should be positioned about 1/64 inch behind the blade.*

piece of paper, so a dollar bill can be used as a spacer. Be careful when doing this. The distance between the blade's gullet, the space between the teeth during the cutting process, and the front of the guide block should be about ¹⁄₆₄ inch because the blade will flex backward during the cut (3-29).

Nonmetal replacement guide blocks called Cool Blocks are available. Cool Blocks are fiber blocks that contain a dry lubricant that greatly decreases the friction between the blade and the blocks. This decreases the heat generated by the blade, and thus increases the life of the blade.

Another advantage of using Cool Blocks is that they can be placed in contact with the blade. This decreases blade twist and deflection, and improves the accuracy of the band-saw cut. Cool

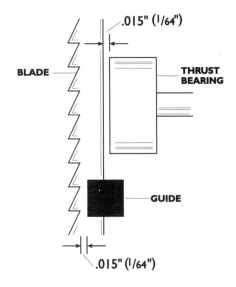

.015" (¹⁄₆₄")

BLADE

THRUST BEARING

GUIDE

.015" (¹⁄₆₄")

3-29. *When the saw has stopped cutting, the blade will spring back to its original position. When adjusting the guides, make sure that the distance between the back of the blade's gullet and the guide is the same as the distance between the blade and the thrust bearing.*

Blocks are essential for narrow blades such as 1/16-inch blades because they cannot destroy the very small teeth the way metal blocks can.

ADJUSTMENT TECHNIQUES FOR NARROW BLADES

Band saws can use blades that are only ⅟₁₆ inch wide. These blades make extremely tight turns similar to those made by an expensive scroll-saw blade. A band saw that can make very tight turns has an advantage in that it can cut much faster, especially in thick, hard wood. That is why these narrow blades are very popular among band-saw users.

To use the narrower blades successfully, these steps will have to be followed. First, replace the metal guides with nonmetal ones. Cool Blocks seem to work best. Place the blocks even with the front of the blade (3-30). Next, as discussed in Preserving Blade Life on pages 51 to 59, round the back of the blade. Also, use center-tracking to track the blade. Keep the top guide assembly about an inch above the work. This will allow the blade to flex rearwards slightly during the cut, thus ensuring that the blade will not be forced to make a sharp angle under the top thrust bearing. The thrust bearing should rest against the back of the blade with no space between the bearing and the blade. (Some experienced band-saw users push the blade about a ⅟₆₄ of an inch forward of the thrust bearings.) This gives the narrow blade added support (3-31).

Blades ⅛ and ⅟₁₆ inch wide last significantly longer when the guide is raised about an inch above the workpiece. However, this exposes about an inch of blade, which could be a potential hazard, so be especially cautious. It may be helpful to fabricate an extension on the guard.

3-30. This band saw is fitted with a ⅟₁₆-inch-wide blade and Cool Blocks. Cool Blocks are replacement nonmetal guide blocks that allow the use of small blades and prolong normal blade life. One of the patented ingredients is graphite, which lubricates the blade.

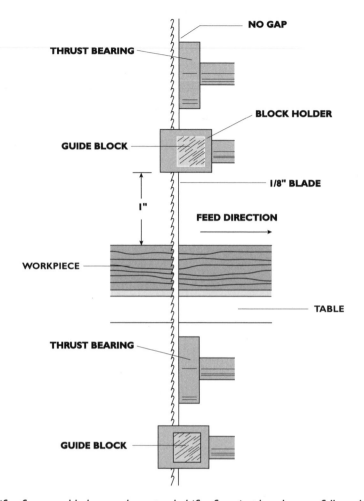

3-31. *The life of narrow blades can be extended if a few simple rules are followed. When a narrow blade such as a ¹/8- or ¹/16-inch blade is being used, the top guide should be kept about an inch above the workpiece. This will allow the blade to flex rearwards slightly during the cut. Cool Blocks should be used because with these blade guides there is less destructive blade heat generated. This is especially important with narrow blades because there is less metal to act as a heat conductor. The cooler the blade, the longer it will last.*

CHAPTER 4

Cutting Techniques

General Cutting Guidelines

When making any type of cut with a band saw, pay attention to the following guidelines:

1. Plan the saw cuts before making them. There are some situations that it is best to avoid, such as having to back out of long, curved cuts. This can cause the blade to move forward off the saw wheels. If the blade has to be backed off the workpiece, turn the saw off first. The top wheel can also be tilted backward slightly (4-1). This will decrease the likelihood of the saw blade coming forward off the wheels when it is backed out.

2. Feed the work gently into the blade. Do not force the work or bend or twist the blade. Remember that when a turn is being made, especially a tight turn, the wood may be fed forward. A gentle, smooth rhythm will provide the best results.

3. In most sawing situations, a cutting line should be followed. A pencil line works best because it does not leave a permanent stain, and it can be erased. Saw near the outside of the line, but not on it. This way, the line will still be intact if the edge is sanded or planed, and the desired shape can still be seen.

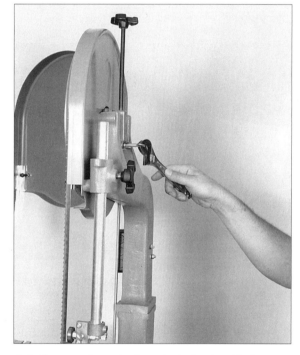

4-1. One way to make it easier to back a blade out of a cut is to tilt the top wheel backward slightly. Turn the saw off before doing this.

4. Both hands should be used to feed the wood into the blade (4-2). They should be positioned on opposite sides of the workpiece. The hands should never be crossed. If the sawer is in an awkward position, he or she should keep one hand on the work and move the other hand. Fingers should be kept away from the pencil line, especially at the end of the cut.

4-2. *The proper cutting technique for making a curved cut. The workpiece is slowly rotated. As the cut progresses, one hand is slowly moved to the back of the workpiece. A thumb is used to move the piece forward. Sawing is done near, but not on the pencil line. The final edge is produced by sanding to the line.*

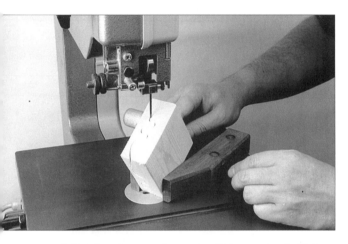

4-3. *A hand-screw clamp should be used to hold the workpiece when it doesn't rest flat on the table.*

5. A jig or clamp should be used to hold odd-shaped or small pieces during the sawing process (4-3). Small pieces are more dangerous to cut than large ones because the operator's fingers are closer to the blade.

Cutting Curves

CURVE-CUTTING GUIDELINES

One advantage the band saw has over other power tools is that it can cut curves in both thick and thin wood. A curved cut is possible because the workpiece can be rotated around the narrow blade.

When the workpiece is turned sharply, the back of the blade rubs against the saw kerf. This is the smallest turn that it is possible to make. If the workpiece is rotated past this point, the blade body will start to twist. This should be avoided because twisting the blade shortens its life. To prevent the blade from twisting, the workpiece must be fed forward into the blade during a sharp turn, and a blade of the appropriate width should be used. (Refer to the blade-width chart on page 35 to determine the proper blade width for specific cuts.)

It is important that when turns are being made they be planned for ahead of time. Planning helps to minimize the wasted material and decrease the difficulty of the cut. For example, when making a piece that has parallel curves, it is possible to make one curved cut and then glue the separate pieces back together with their flat sides in contact with each other. This saves time and material, and increases the accuracy of the cut. If the grain of the different pieces is chosen carefully, the glue line will be nearly impossible to see.

CURVE-CUTTING TECHNIQUES

Cutting curves presents challenges different from other cutting techniques. Below are techniques to use when cutting curves. They will prove helpful in specific situations.

Using a Rip Fence to Cut Curved Multiple Pieces

When cutting multiple pieces with parallel curves, it is possible to use the rip fence to space the width of the workpiece. A rip fence is an accessory used to control the saw when a cut is being ripped, that is, made along the grain of the wood. The workpiece should touch the fence about ¼ inch in front of the saw blade (4-4 and 4-5). This technique allows the operator to make multiple pieces that

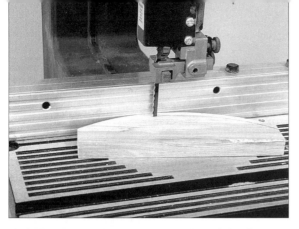

4-4. *The distance between the blade and the fence determines the width of the workpiece. Keep the workpiece against the fence when making the cut.*

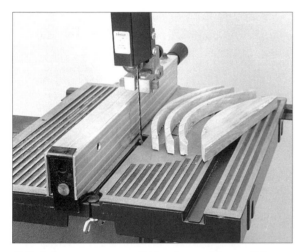

4-5. *It is easy to cut multiple pieces with parallel curves if the rip fence is used to space the width of the workpiece. Refer to Making Multiple Pieces on pages 95 and 96 for more information.*

are exactly the same size with very little effort. It works on small and large workpieces.

Refer to Making a Rip Fence on pages 99 and 100 for information on making a rip fence.

Single-Point Technique for Curves

As discussed in the previous section, the rip fence can be used as a rotation point for determining the width of the workpiece. This technique works well if the piece curves gently in one direction. If the piece curves in several directions, a similar technique is used, except that the rotation

To use the single-point technique, clamp the pointed stick to the fence or the table (4-6). If the curve to be cut is a gentle curve, use a stick with a pointed point. Locate the point about ½ inch in front of the blade. Hold the edge of the workpiece against the point. The piece has to be "fish-tailed" or angled into the blade at the correct angle.

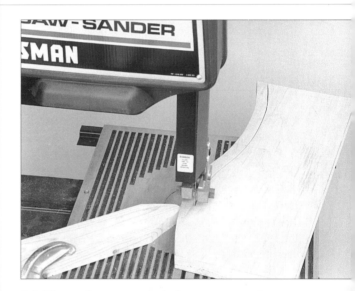

4-6. *The single-point method of cutting curves. Begin the cut with the corner of the workpiece against the point. Continue the cut by putting light pressure against the point. Hold the workpiece against the point and shove it into the blade.*

This technique does require some skill and concentration. It is particularly useful on pieces with multiple curves, such as chair backs. It is also useful on small objects with multiple curves, such as band-sawed boxes. When the single-point technique is used for small objects or tight curves, the point on the stick should be sharp rather than rounded.

Release Cuts

A release cut is used to prevent the band-saw operator from getting into situations in which

CUTTING CURVES **85**

the workpiece can't be retracted from the blade. A release cut is made to meet with the end of a long cut. It is used so that the waste piece can be easily separated from the workpiece (4-7 and 4-8).

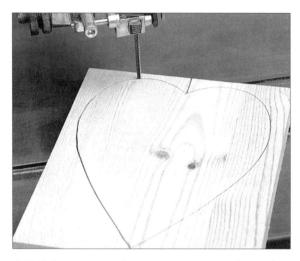

4-7. *Release cuts make it easier to retract the workpiece. They should be made as straight as possible. The cut path is marked using a ruler or square. Then the release cut is made. The second cut, shown here, should end at the release cut.*

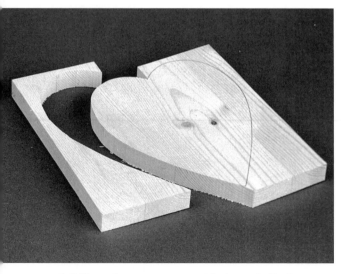

4-8. *The release cut meets with the end of a long cut. Because the workpiece was accurately squared, the release cut and the edge of the board are parallel. The second cut intersects with the release cut, which frees the waste piece.*

Turning Holes

Turning holes, like release cuts, are used so that the waste piece can be easily separated from the workpiece (4-9). Turning holes are drilled at key positions in the workpiece. They can serve as a smooth curve in a pattern (4-10). The holes and the straight cuts are made first (4-11 and 4-12). The rest of the material is the waste material.

Turning holes are also used at key locations to give the operator more space to rotate the workpiece around the saw blade. They help the operator cut out complex patterns more quickly.

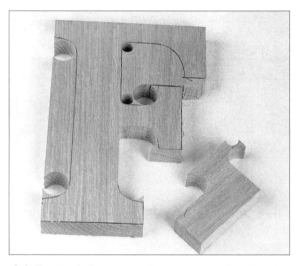

4-9. *Turning holes are another way to easily separate small waste pieces from the workpiece.*

4-10. *A project in which turning holes are used.*

4-11. The next step is to drill the turning holes. The holes should be large enough so that the workpiece can be rotated freely around the blade.

4-12. After the turning holes are drilled, the straight cuts are made. The straight cuts release the waste material.

Cutting a Square Inside Corner

Unless a narrow blade is being used, it is difficult to make a square inside corner. In this situation, it is best to make as many straight cuts as possible into the corners. Then back up and make a turn. Finally, cut the waste out of the corners (4-13).

Making Circular Cuts

Circular cuts are often used when sharp curves have to be made. In such cases, it is useful to cut past the corner and make a circular cut in the waste area. Continue the cut into the corner. This cut will function like a release cut. Then back up the workpiece and make another cut

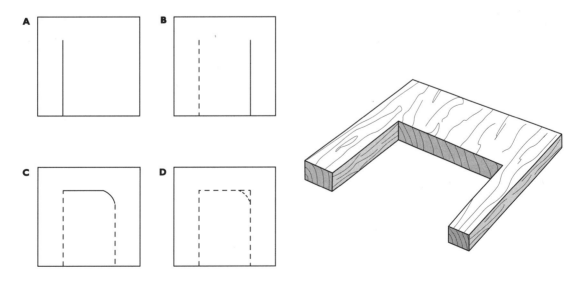

4-13. How to remove waste from a square area. Make the straight cuts first, as shown in A and B. B is a release cut for the curved cut, shown in C. D is a straight cut that removes the waste piece from the corner.

along the opposite side. This cut will release the waste (4-14 and 4-15).

4-14. *When making a sharp curve, it is often useful to make a circular cut. These cuts function like release cuts, releasing the waste.*

4-15. *Continue the cut into the corner. It will release a half circle of waste, which will fall through the throat plate into the band saw. It is important that the waste piece falls opposite the bottom wheel. If the waste piece falls between the blade and the wheel, it can break or cause kinks in the wheel.*

Nibbling

When a pattern is being sawn out, the large pieces of waste are removed first. Nibbling is the technique often used on tight curves in which the blade is used to remove small pieces of material. When the small waste pieces are cut away, this creates room for the blade, so that the workpiece can be rotated without having to twist the blade body (4-16 to 4-18).

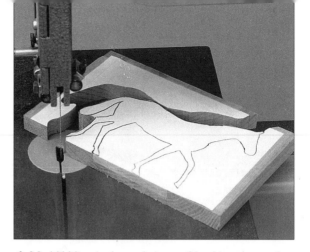

4-16. *Nibbling is the technique of backing the workpiece up and making multiple cuts that are the width of the blade. This creates enough room so that the workpiece can be rotated without the need to twist the blade. This technique is useful in situations such as cutting patterns, which is shown here.*

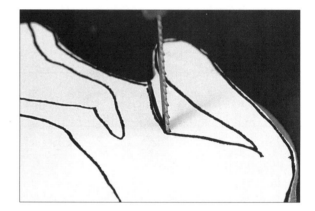

4-17. *The corner is too square to allow the blade to rotate, so the first step is to make a straight cut into the corner. Then the workpiece is backed up and multiple cuts the width of the blade are made, as shown here.*

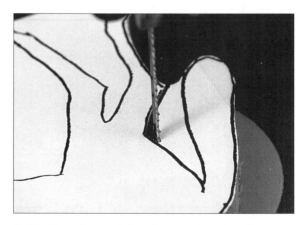

4-18. *Next, the workpiece is rotated so that the blade is in line with the pencil line.*

Making Tight Curves with Wide Blades

In certain situations a tight curve will have to be made, but the operator will not want to change to a narrower blade. Tight curves using a wide blade can be made with a series of straight cuts. Inside curves can be made with a series of release cuts (4-19).

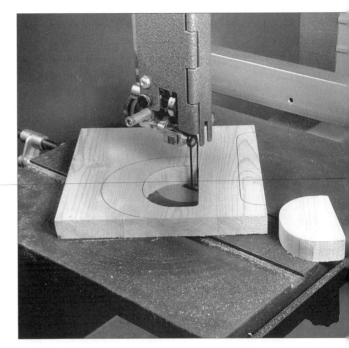

4-20. *Making interior cuts. Here the letter P is being cut out. The straight entry cut is made using the fence. Then the waste is removed.*

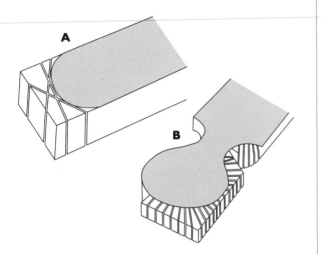

4-19. *Inside curves can be made with a wide blade via a series of straight cuts, as shown in A. As shown in B, outside curves can also be made with a series of straight cuts.*

Making Interior Cuts

Wood-cutting band saws are not designed to do interior-cutting. Metal-cutting band saws often have welders, so the blade can be threaded through a hole and rewelded. With some planning, interior cuts can be made and then sanded with a drum sander. A good example is the letter P (4-20). Make the entry cut by using the fence and remove the waste. Make the rest of the cuts, but leave a square corner to support the clamp. Glue the entering cut. After it dries, cut off the square corner. It takes only a few minutes to make the interior cut and to reglue it (4-21).

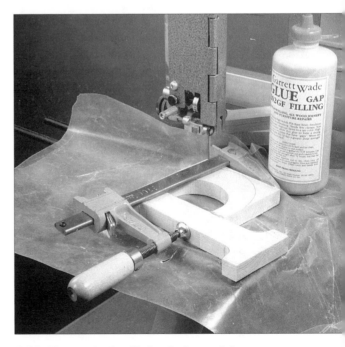

4-21. *The saw kerf is filled with glue and then clamped. A corner is left uncut. This makes the kerf easier to clamp.*

Intarsia and Marquetry Techniques

Two pieces with different designs are often used next to each other as a decorative motif. When solid wood is used, this technique is called intarsia (4-22). When veneer is used, it is referred to as marquetry.

When the techniques of marquetry and intarsia are used, two mating pieces usually have to be simultaneously cut. When the cuts are long or gentle curves, the two pieces will fit exceptionally well if the blade and table are at 90 degrees to each other. One piece is placed on top of the other and then both are cut at the same time (4-23 to 4-25). Then the pieces are glued together in such a way that the top piece mates with the bottom piece (4-26).

If the curves are tight or the design is small, the matching pieces will fit better if the table is slightly angled. This angle accurately helps to compensate for the wood lost to the saw kerf. Experiment with scrap wood to get the right angle. This angle will depend on the blade's width and the thickness of the wood.

Table 4-1 will help a band-saw operator determine the right degree of table tilt needed to create a tight fit. It was created by engineer Beau Lowerr, from Milwaukee, Wisconsin.

TABLE 4-1.

KERF	"Background" Wood Thickness (in hundreds of an inch)				
	0.125	0.250	0.375	0.500	0.750
	DEGREES OF TABLE TILT FROM HORIZONTAL				
0.015"	6.9	3.4			
0.016"	7.4	3.7			
0.017"	7.8	3.9			
0.018"	8.3	4.1			
0.019"	8.7	4.4	2.9		
0.020"		4.6	3.1		
0.021"		4.8	3.		
0.022"		5.0	3.4		
0.023"		5.3	3.5		
0.024"		5.5	3.7		
0.025"		5.7	3.8	2.9	1.9
0.026"			4.0	3.0	2.0
0.027"			4.1	3.1	2.1
0.028"			4.3	3.2	2.1
0.029"			4.4	3.3	2.2
0.030"			4.6	3.4	2.3

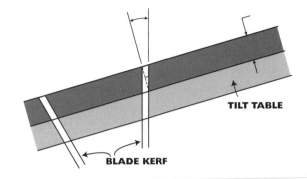

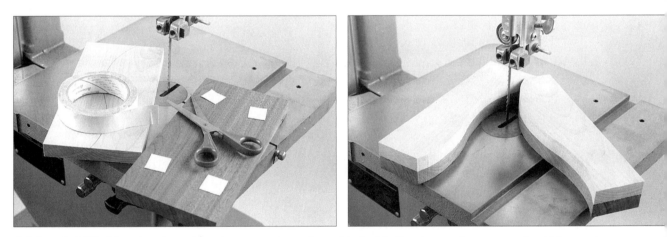

4-22 (above). *An project made using intarsia.*
4-23 (right). *The top piece of wood mates with the bottom piece after the angled saw cut is made.*

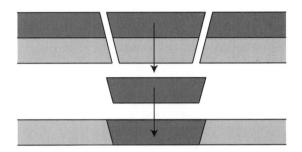

4-24 and 4-25. *After the pieces have been taped together with double-faced tape, the saw cut should be made.*

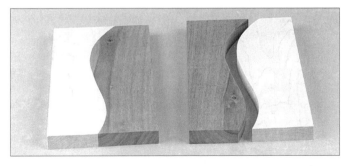

4-26. *If the saw cut is a gentle curve, the opposite pieces are glued and fitted tightly together.*

Scroll-Sawing

Not too long ago a scroll saw was used with narrow blades to make tight turns. This procedure was called scroll-sawing. With the introduction of 1/16-inch-wide blades for use on a band saw and nonmetallic guide blocks, it is possible to do scroll-saw work with a band saw. The 1/16-inch-wide band-saw blades make extremely tight turns similar to those made by an expensive scroll-saw blade (4-27).

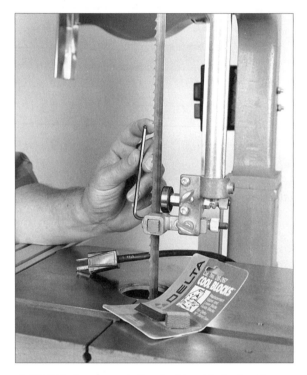

4-27. *This band saw is fitted with a 1/16-inch-wide blade and Cool Blocks. Cool Blocks are replacement guide blocks that allow the use of narrow blades and prolong blade life. The blade and the front of the blocks are aligned with each other.*

A 1/16-inch-wide band-saw blade has a very fine pitch (many teeth per inch), to ensure that the final cut will be smooth. It can also make very accurate straight cuts that would be very difficult, if not impossible, to make with a scroll saw. These narrow band-saw blades can also be used to make cuts in very thick material. This can be useful when the band saw is used to make name signs or a variety of other products (4-28).

In order for these narrow blades to be used successfully, changes will have to be made in the standard adjustment procedure. It is necessary to replace the metal guide with nonmetal ones such as Cool Blocks. Place these blocks just behind the blade's gullets.

4-28. *A 1/16-inch band-saw blade cuts much faster than a scroll-saw blade, particularly in thick, hard wood such as the 2-inch-thick hard maple shown here.*

As discussed on pages 58 and 59, the back of a narrow band-saw blade should be rounded. On narrow blades such as 1/8- or 1/16-inch-wide blades, the pressure on the back of the blade may bring the blade forward off the front of the wheels. To prevent this, feed wood into the blade during the rounding process. Pass the wood underneath the elevated stone. This keeps the blade in contact with the thrust bearing.

When using narrow blades, use center tracking to track the blade. (Refer to Tracking Procedure on pages 68 to 76 for information on center-tracking.) Keep the top guide assembly about an inch above the work. This will allow the blade to flex rearwards slightly during the cut. This eliminates the possibility that the blade will be forced to make a sharp angle under the top thrust bearing. However, this exposes about an inch of blade, which could be dangerous, so be very careful. The thrust bearing should rest against the blade with no space between the bearing and the blade. This gives the small blades added support.

Blades that are ⅛- and ¹⁄₁₆-inch wide last significantly longer when the guide is raised. Some experienced woodworkers move the thrust bearings forward about ¹⁄₆₄ inch to ensure that the back of the blade always contacts the thrust bearings.

"Cut-and-Glue" Scroll-Sawing

A narrow blade can be used on a band saw to make inside cuts. This is done by cutting two halves of the piece and then gluing them together. This is referred to as the "cut and glue" technique (4-29).

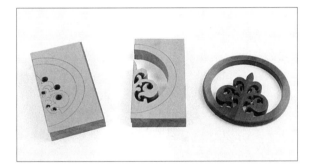

4-29. The "cut-and-glue" technique consists of cutting two halves of a workpiece and then gluing them together.

The cut-and-glue technique has advantages. Both sides of the pattern are cut at the same time, so sawing time is saved. The more complex the pattern, the greater the savings in time. Another advantage is that because the two sides are cut at the same time, they are perfectly symmetrical. This is an important factor because no matter how well someone scroll-saws, it is extremely difficult to make two halves of a pattern exactly the same.

Gluing the two pieces together may require creative techniques, although the time it takes to

glue them is not nearly as great as the time it would take to cut the two halves individually. When gluing, dowels can be used to locate the two halves in relation to each other. Use double-faced tape or clothespins to hold the two interior halves together (4-30 and 4-31).

4-30. After the pieces are cut, double-faced tape is used to hold them together. Rubber cement is used to attach the pattern to the piece. Notice that turning holes, as discussed on pages 86 and 87, are being used here. They make it easier for the operator to cut the pattern. The last step consists of removing the large piece of waste. A ⅛-inch-wide blade is being used in this situation

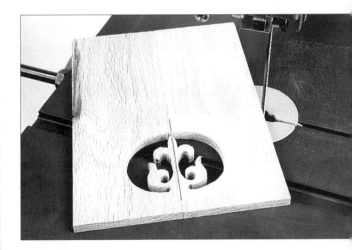

4-31. The completed two halves of the piece. The pattern is removed, and then the pieces are glued together. A clothespin makes a good clamp for the two narrow pieces inside the pattern. A rubber band can also be used.

Making Cabriole Legs

Cabriole legs are curved furniture legs that have ornamental feet. They are commonly used by furniture-makers, but beginners may find making them intimidating. Making cabriole legs is actually quite simple if the correct sequence is followed. It is also important that the pattern is laid out properly. Since sets of four legs are often made, pattern layout may become confusing. Remember to use the same pattern on two adjacent sides. The knees and feet should be pointing toward each other (4-32).

Here is the step-by-step sequence for making cabriole legs: Cut the straight lines first. Then cut the backs of the legs (4-33 and 4-34). Make the long cuts last. Make sure there is enough stock so

---

MAKING CABRIOLE LEGS

4-32. Making a cabriole leg. Cabriole legs are furniture legs that have ornamental feet. When making a cabriole leg, use the same pattern on the two adjacent sides.

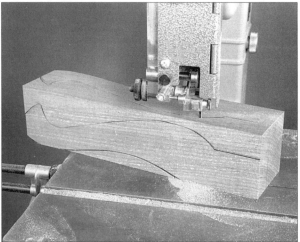

4-33. First, the straight lines are cut. Then the back of the leg is cut and the heels cut off, as shown here. A flat area should be left between the heels and the back of the leg. This area can be rounded later.

4-34. If the waste piece for the back of the leg is placed under the workpiece, the workpiece will not tip off the edge of the table.

that the pattern is not cut through on the outside of the leg. Also, leave about ¹⁄₁₆ of an inch of material between the cut and the straight release cut. This technique is called a "hinge cut." If it is done correctly, the wood will open, making it easy to back the blade out of the cut (4-35). If this ¹⁄₁₆ of material is accidentally cut, the pieces can be taped back on. It is important that the

long piece is well-positioned because it has the pattern for the next cut on the adjacent side.

Rotate the workpiece to expose the pattern and finish the cut. Break the hinge cut; this will expose the completed leg (4-36). Sanding the leg takes a minimal amount of time if an inflatable drum sander is used. The drum sander can be adjusted with air pressure so that it fits the shape of the leg.

MAKING CABRIOLE LEGS (CONTINUED)

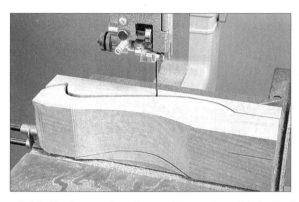

4-35. Don't complete the cut. Leave about ¹⁄₁₆ inch of material between the cut and the straight release cut. This "hinge" cut allows the kerf to be opened, which makes it easier to back the blade out. This allows the adjacent pattern to remain intact.

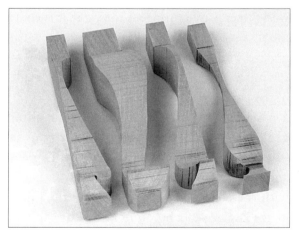

4-36. The leg and the three waste pieces. The leg can be easily sanded with an inflatable drum sander.

Making Multiple Pieces

The band saw is often used to make multiple pieces. This can be accomplished with a number of different techniques. In one technique, a stop can be used when multiple pieces of the same size are being crosscut. Another technique, called "stack-sawing," consists of sandwiching multiple

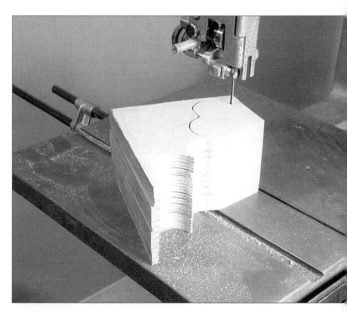

4-37 and 4-38 (following page). Stack-sawing multiple pieces. These pieces of plywood are held together with rubber padding compound, a material used to make tablets. Rubber padding compound is usually available from office-supply stores. It is a rubber, liquid-like substance that is painted on. It dries quickly. Rubber cement also works well. Tape, glue, screws, and nails can also be used to hold a stack of workpieces securely.

pieces together and cutting them (4-37 and 4-38). Other techniques consist of slicing thin pieces off thick stock (4-39) and pattern-sawing, in which a solid pattern is attached to the workpiece and cut. Pattern-sawing is discussed on pages 127 and 128.

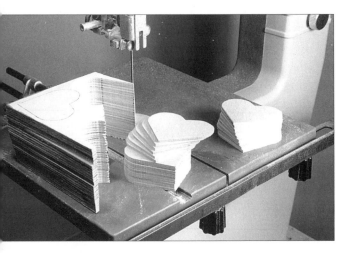

4-38. *A complete stack of hearts that are exactly the same size.*

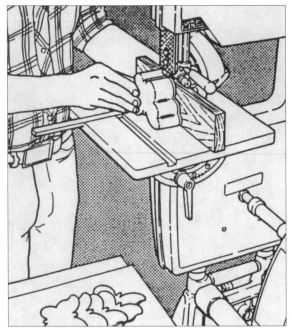

4-39. *Slicing thin pieces off thick stock is another method of making multiple pieces. (Drawing courtesy of Shopsmith.)*

Making Straight Cuts

The band saw can make a variety of straight cuts, including crosscuts, rip cuts, resawing cuts, bevel cuts, cuts made to round stock, taper cuts, and cuts used to make tenons and dovetails. All these cuts are detailed in the following sections in this chapter.

When straight band-saw cuts are made, the work is either fed into the blade freehand or a jig or fixture is used to control the workpiece. To maintain consistency and accuracy, use a jig or fixture if possible. The fixtures most often used are the miter gauge, the rip fence, and the taper jig. In special situations, a fixture that slides in the band saw's miter slot is used.

Refer to pages 129 to 148 for more information on building and using miter gauges, rip fences, taper jigs, and miter jigs when performing the cutting techniques discussed in the following sections in this chapter.

CROSSCUTTING

A crosscut is a cut made across the grain of the workpiece. A miter gauge is the jig that is commonly used when a band saw is being used to make a variety of crosscuts (4-40). The head of the miter gauge is adjusted to the desired angle of the cut.

A standard crosscut is made with the miter gauge set at 90 degrees. A bevel crosscut is made with the miter gauge set at 90 degrees and the table angled. A miter cut is made with the table set at 90 degrees and the miter gauge angled. A compound miter cut is made with both the miter gauge and the table angled (4-41).

A rip fence can also be used to make straight

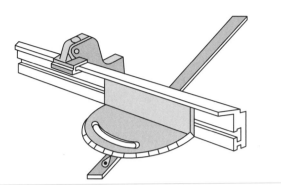

1. CROSSCUT
2. BEVELED CROSSCUT
3. MITER CUT
4. COMPOUND MITER CUT

4-40. *These straight crosscuts can be made with a miter gauge.*

4-41. *A compound miter crosscut is made with both the table and the miter gauge angled. Clamping the workpiece to the miter gauge prevents the work from sliding.*

4-42. *A squaring jig, which features a plane-type handle, is being used with the rip fence to make an accurate crosscut. The more teeth there are on the blade, the better the quality of the crosscut.*

crosscuts. It is particularly useful on wide boards. A squaring jig can be used with a rip fence to make an accurate crosscut. A squaring jig is a square piece of plywood with a knob or handle in the middle of it. The workpiece is held against the squaring jig, and the adjacent side of the jig is held against the fence. The jig and the workpiece are moved into the blade as a unit (4-42).

If many straight crosscuts will be made, use a narrow blade with standard teeth. A wide blade usually works best for straight cuts, but wide blades usually have skip or hook teeth, which are not the best choice for crosscutting. Wide blades with standard teeth can be ordered, but it is easier to use a narrow blade with standard teeth.

When making crosscuts, the best blade to use is one with a pitch of 12 to 14 teeth per inch. One-eighth-inch-wide blades usually have a pitch of 12 to 14 TPI. Because narrow blades flex rearwards during the cut, they make very accurate cuts.

The accuracy of narrow blades such as ⅛- and 1/16-inch-wide blades can be increased if the guide is raised about an inch above the workpiece. This allows the blade to flex rearwards in a gentle arc, which exposes the blade under the guide. However, raising the guide is potentially dangerous, so by very careful. Cool Blocks, which are non-metallic replacement guide blocks, can be used in contact with the blade and increase the accuracy of the cut by decreasing the blade's sideways deflection.

RIP CUTS

A rip cut is a straight cut made with the grain of the wood (4-43). Other cuts made with the grain of the wood are bevel, taper, and resaw cuts.

There are two frequently used techniques for making straight band-saw rip cuts. One technique is to use a single point to guide the work (4-44). The reason for using a single point is that the saw may tend to cut at a slight angle. This is often called "lead." The single point allows the operator to feed the wood into the blade at a slight angle, which compensates for blade lead.

With a little practice, satisfactory results can be obtained with the single-point method. Because this technique requires constant attention, it is not recommended for a great volume of work.

The second technique used to make straight rip cuts consists of using the rip fence as a guide (4-45). If a great deal of cutting will be done or a curved rip fence will be used, adjust the angle of the rip fence to correspond with blade lead. This is a fairly simple, quick procedure that consists of the following steps:

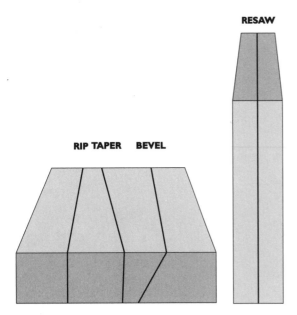

4-43. *The four most common cuts made with the grain are rip, bevel, taper, and resaw cuts. Bevel, taper, and resaw cuts are discussed in other sections in this chapter.*

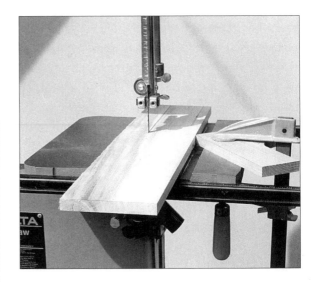

4-44. *The single-point method of making rip cuts allows the wood to be fed into the blade at a slight angle. This compensates for blade "lead," which is the blade's tendency to cut at a slight angle.*

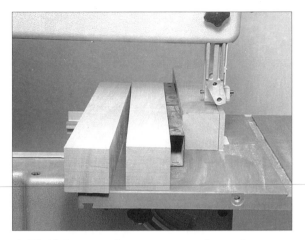

4-45. *Making straight rip cuts using the rip fence. Most often, the distance between the rip fence and the blade determines the size of the workpiece. This is called the "inside." In this case, the waste piece is the piece on the side of the blade opposite the fence. Shown here is the usual procedure for making multiple pieces. All of these pieces are being cut on the inside.*

1. Make a straight pencil mark on the edge of the mark.

2. Feed the wood into the blade. Make the cuts next to the pencil mark. If the blade is leading, angle it slightly to ensure that it cuts along the pencil mark (4-46).

3. Stop the cut in the middle of the board and mark the angle on the table with a pencil. This is the angle at which the blade is leading, and thus the best angle at which to feed work into the blade.

4. Loosen the bolts which hold the rip fence and adjust the angle of the fence to correspond with the mark on the table (4-47). In fact, each time the blade is changed it is a good idea to check and possibly adjust the angle of the fence.

Making a Rip Fence

Most band saws have rip fences as optional pieces of equipment. However, rip fences may not offer such an option. A user-made rip fence for making rip cuts or resawings can be made by

4-46. *Feed the wood into the blade on the pencil mark to make a test cut. To make a straight cut, the workpiece may have to be angled. The angle shown here is the one at which the saw blade cuts best.*

4-47. *The fence bolts are loosened with a wrench, and the angle of the fence is changed so that it corresponds to the angle of the test cut.*

using two pieces of plywood secured at a 90-degree angle (4-48 and 4-49). A curved auxiliary wood fence can be used for techniques such as resawing, as discussed in the following section.

Refer to Rip Fences on pages 131 to 133 for more information on user-made rip fences.

RESAWING

Resawing is the process of cutting a thick board in half along its width (4-50). When the board is resawed and the two pieces are lying flat, next to each other, they appear to be mirror images of each other. When the two boards are glued

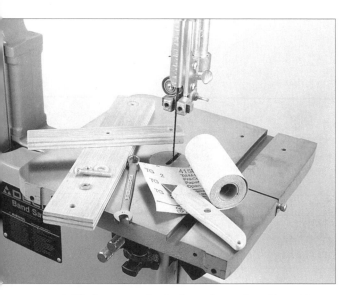

4-48. *A user-made rip fence. It consists of two pieces of plywood secured at a 90-degree angle. Attaching a small piece of sandpaper to the top of the small piece of plywood will prevent the two pieces from rotating in relationship with each other.*

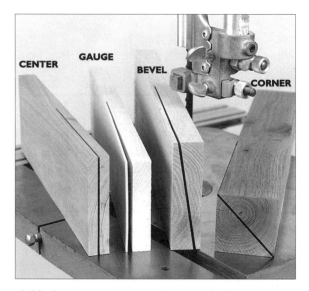

4-50. *Resawing is cutting a board in half along its width. Shown from left to right are center-, gauge-, bevel-, and corner-sawing methods of resawing.*

4-49. *The fence is held in place with a clamp.*

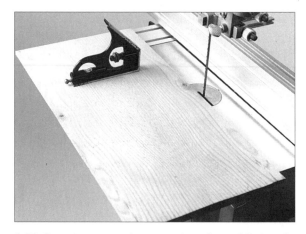

4-51. *Resawing exposes the two inside surfaces of the board. The two surfaces are mirror images of each other. When the two matching halves are glued together, it is called bookmatching. The board shown here has been bookmatched.*

together, it is called "bookmatching" (4-51). Bookmatching greatly enhances the character of a piece and is useful on all surfaces that are flat, such as tabletops and doors.

The following sections on resawing describe which blades are needed, proper tensioning procedures for the blades, and resawing techniques that include the use of a curved-wood auxiliary fence.

Choosing the Blade

Cutting thick stock puts maximum strain on both the blade and the band saw, so it is recommended that the widest blade for the saw be used. For a band saw with wheels up to 14 inches in diameter, the largest recommended blade is a ½-inch-wide hook blade with three teeth per inch (4-52). This blade's width offers maximum beam strength, which is the ability of the blade to resist deflection. Its hook teeth cut aggressively, and its large gullet can carry the waste through the stock. The blade has to be sharp, so begin with a new or a resharpened blade. As the blade dulls, its cutting speed will slow and its tendency to lead or wander will increase.

4-52. *A ¹/₂-inch-wide hook blade with three teeth per inch is the largest blade that can be used to cut thick stock.*

Tensioning the Blade

After choosing the blade, the next step is to tension it. One of the most debatable aspects of band-saw use is how much the blade should be tensioned. If the saw is well-tuned and adjusted (refer to Chapter 3 for tuning and adjustment procedures), and a sharp blade is being used, the blade should be able to slice off veneers with the tension scale set at the ½-inch setting for the ½-inch blade. It may be helpful to increase tension slightly as the blade dulls.

Remember, however, that increasing a blade's tension will not magically solve all cutting problems. It can actually aggravate problems by pulling or twisting the frame out of proper alignment. Also, the bearings and shafts wear out rapidly if the saw is overtensioned.

Resawing with a Curved Wood Auxiliary Fence

Before resawing, or making any cuts for that matter, check that the table is square to the blade (4-53) and that the fence is square to the table (4-54). If the blade and the fence are both square to the table, they should be parallel with each other.

There are two frequently used techniques for making straight band-saw cuts such as those involved in resawing. One technique is to use the rip fence as a guide. Another technique is to use a single point to guide the work. (Refer to Rip Cuts on pages 98 to 100 for more information on the single-point technique.) To resaw thick wood as discussed here, a combination of these two techniques that contains the advantages of both techniques is used. A curved wood auxiliary shop-made fence is attached to the standard rip fence.

The curved fence should be about six inches

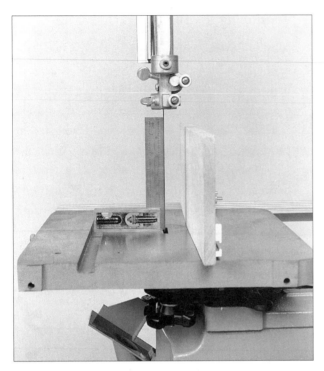

4-53. Before resawing, check that the table is square to the blade.

4-54. Also check that the fence is square to the table.

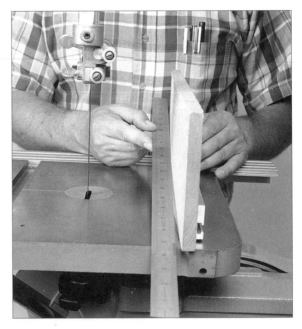

4-55. The six-inch-high auxiliary resawing fence is about 1/4 inch thicker in the middle than it is at its two ends.

high and the length of the rip fence (4-55). It is attached to the rip fence with screws or bolts, and is designed to be roughly ¼ inch thicker in the middle than on the two ends.

A jointer is used to make the curved fence. Use a stop block clamped to the jointer to efficiently remove the material (4-56). The stop block should be located less than half the length of the fence from the out-feed table of the jointer. The middle of the board should rest on the out-feed table before the cut. Use a wide push stick to safely cut the taper. A sharp hand plane is used to give the fence its final smooth shape. The curved fence is then screwed to the rip fence.

The thickest part of the curved fence should be aligned with the band-saw blade. As wood is fed into the blade, light pressure is exerted against the fence at a point right in front of the blade.

One advantage of the curved fence is that it allows the feed direction to be adjusted during the cut. Each board has a different density and may require

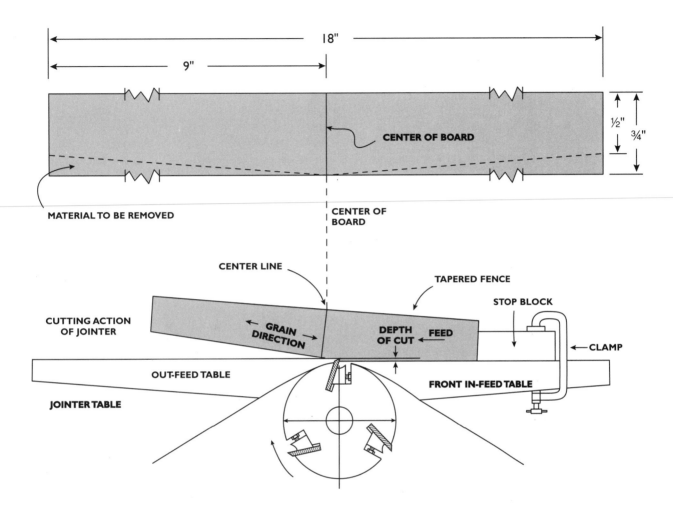

4-56. *Using a jointer to cut the curved fence. This takes a little work. Using a stop block that is clamped to the jointer removes most of the material. The stop block should be located less than half the length of the fence from the out-feed table of the jointer. The middle of the board should rest on the out-feed table before the cut. Use a wide push stick to safely cut the taper.*

a slightly different feed direction. There is another advantage. Occasionally when a board is being resawed, it separates and starts to spread apart. The curved fence allows room for this expansion.

As with all new techniques, when resawing with a curved fence some experimentation is suggested.

Resawing Technique

When resawing, the feed rate is very important. As a general rule, the slower the better. It is imperative that the blade does not deflect or twist because once it starts wandering, it is virtually impossible to get it to cut straight again.

Keep pressure against the fence just behind the blade (4-57). Do not apply pressure near the blade, for safety reasons. This is because the blade could deflect and cut through the side of the workpiece. Good resawing is the result of proper machine alignment, correct blade use, and a slow, steady feed rate. If these factors are followed, it is possible to cut a uniform piece of veneer (4-58).

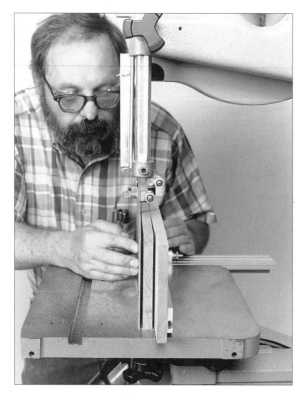

4-57. *When resawing, feed the workpiece slowly, applying pressure against the fence just behind the blade. For safety reasons, never apply pressure next to the blade.*

4-58. *Proper band-saw alignment, a sharp 1/2 inch-wide 3 TPI blade, and a slow, steady feed rate yield a uniform piece of veneer.*

BEVEL CUTS

Bevel cuts are cuts made with the table tilted (4-59). One way of making bevel cuts is to use the rip fence on the downhill side of the blade so that the workpiece cannot slide off the table. Another approach consists of using a V-shaped block to support the workpiece rather than tilting the table.

CUTTING ROUND STOCK

When round stock is being cut, it is vital that the cut be made through the middle of the workpiece. If the cut is located anywhere other than the middle of the board, the down-

4-59. *Bevels are cut with the table tilted. The high fence and the tilted table cradle the workpiece.*

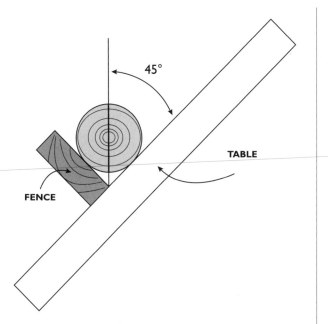

4-60. *A rip fence and tilted table can be used to rip round stock. The cut has to be made in the middle of the board to prevent it from rotating.*

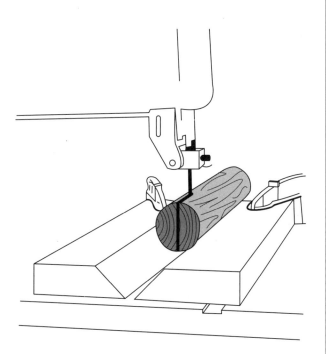

4-61. *A V-shaped block can be used to support the workpiece during the cut.*

ward pressure from the blade will cause the piece to rotate. This rotation often breaks the blade. A V-shaped block can be used to support the workpiece during the cut (4-60 and 4-61).

CUTTING TAPERS

Most tapers are angled cuts made along the grain of the workpiece. They are often used on chair and table legs (4-62). When making tapered cuts on a long piece, use a jig. A user-made or commercial jig can be used.

There are three types of taper-cutting jigs: fixed-angle jig, step jig, and adjustable taper jig. The fixed-angle jig is the simplest one to make (4-63). It is simply an angled piece of wood with a brass screw in one end which pushes the workpiece through the end.

The step jig, a fixture that has three notches or steps, is used to make a taper on one side, opposite sides, or adjacant sides of a workpiece. The jig rides against the rip fence of the saw. The first cut is made with the workpiece resting on the middle or second step (4-64). To make a taper on the opposite side of the workpiece, use the third step on the jig. To make a taper on the adjacent side, rotate the workpiece 90 degrees (4-65).

The step jig is easy to make (4-66). Cut a piece of wood the width of the desired taper. Cut three pieces off the end of the piece and glue them, creating steps about ¼ inch high.

The adjustable taper jig has a hinge on one end and a locking mechanism on the opposite end. This jig can be adjusted to the desired angle. 4-67 shows a commercial version of the jig, but it is easy to make one out of scrap wood.

CUTTING TAPERS

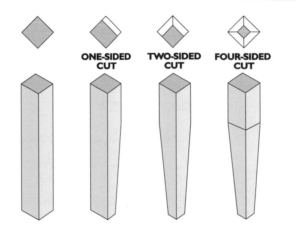

4-62. The three types of tapered cuts: a one-sided cut, a two-sided cut, and a four-sided cut.

4-63. A fixed-angle jig is simply an angled piece of wood with a brass screw in its end that pushes the workpiece through the blade.

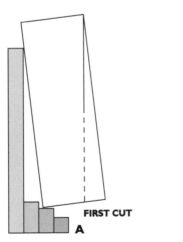
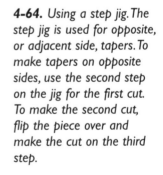

4-64. Using a step jig. The step jig is used for opposite, or adjacent side, tapers. To make tapers on opposite sides, use the second step on the jig for the first cut. To make the second cut, flip the piece over and make the cut on the third step.

FIRST CUT

A

SECOND CUT

B

CUTTING TAPERS (CONTINUED)

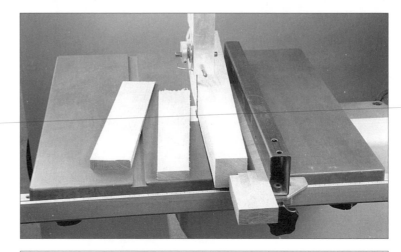

4-65. *To make tapers on adjacent sides using the step taper jig, use the second step on the jig for both cuts. After the first cut, rotate the piece 90 degrees for the second cut.*

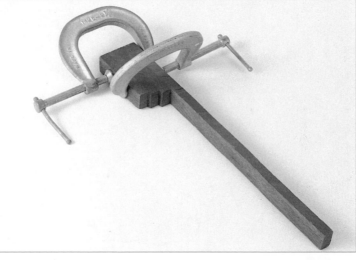

4-66. *The step jig consists of a piece of wood the width of the desired taper and three steps.*

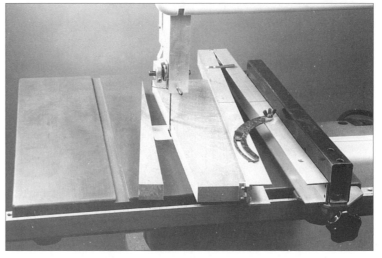

4-67. *This commercially available taper jig is adjustable. It has a taper of one inch per foot.*

MAKING MORTISE-AND-TENON JOINTS

A mortise-and-tenon joint is an extremely strong joint. It is a two-part joint. The mortise is a slot cut into one piece. The tenon is the mating piece that fits into the mortise. Mortise-and-tenon joints are used for frame work such as that used on chairs and tables.

There are several types of mortise-and-tenon joints. As shown in 4-68, they are the through mortise-and-tenon, the blind mortise-and-tenon, the haunched mortise-and-tenon, the stub mortise-and-tenon, and the mitered mortise-and-tenon.

The easiest way to make a mortise is with a plunge router. However, the mortise made with a router requires a tenon that will fit the round corner made by the router bit. One solution is to bevel the tenon corners, that is, cut them so that they are angled (4-69). The 45-degree tenon corner will fit snugly into the round corner. This approach has an advantage in that it allows for

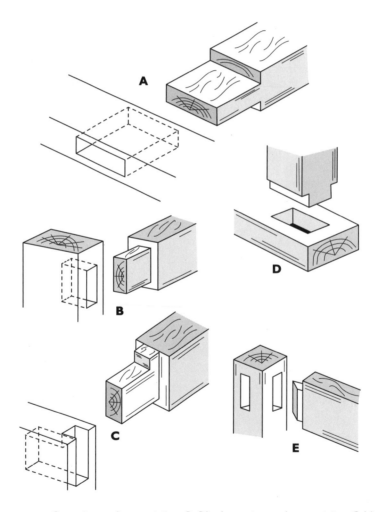

4-68. *Various types of mortise-and-tenon joints. B: Blind mortise-and-tenon joint. C: Haunched mortise-and-tenon joint. D: Stub mortise-and-tenon joint. E: Mitered mortise-and-tenon joint.*

4-69. *The corners on this tenon are beveled. The beveled corners fit the round mortise made by a router bit. The flat surfaces allow for the release of glue much like the flutes on a dowel.*

4-71. *Making rip cuts on the band saw to define the neck of the tenon.*

4-70. *Using a table saw to make crosscuts that define the shoulders of the tenon.*

the escape of captured glue. This is the idea behind the fluted dowel.

The tenon requires two types of cuts: crosscuts and rip cuts. First, a crosscut is used to define the shoulders of the tenon. This can be done on the band saw, but is often done on the

table saw (4-70). Next, rip cuts are used to define the neck of the tenon (4-71). The band saw excels at this type of cut because it is able to cut into corners.

One reason it is often better to make the crosscut for the tenon with a table saw is because the crosscut will be slightly deeper (1/32 inch) than the rip cut. This ensures that the corner cut will be complete, and provides a place for the excess glue.

The setup for making the rip cuts for the tenon is the usual setup for ripping, except that a stop block is used to stop the cut (4-72). If a fence with a microadjuster is used, it will be easier to produce a joint that fits tightly.

Two rip cuts are made to define the neck of the tenon. The first is a narrow rip cut made with the board lying flat. The second is a deep rip cut made on the end of the board (4-73). This is the least crit-

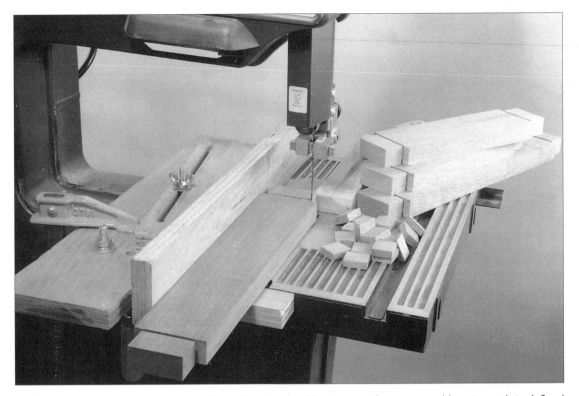

4-72. *The tenon requires two series of cuts. First, its shoulder is cut with a crosscut. Next, its neck is defined with a rip cut. Here the progression of these cuts is shown. The setup for cutting the tenons is similar to that used for rip cuts. Use a stop block to stop the cut. If a fence with a microadjuster is used, it is easier to fit the tenon to the mortise.*

ical of the cuts, especially if the mortise is round.

If the mortise is round, use a 45-degree bevel cut to ensure that the tenon fits into the mortise (4-74). Make the bevel cuts by cutting the opposite corners with the same fence setting.

MAKING DOVETAILS WITH SPACING BLOCKS

With the present emphasis on exposed joinery, hand-cut dovetails have become a symbol of good-quality craftsmanship. The hand-cut method offers unlimited design flexibility. Unfortunately, it is too time-consuming for most professional use and requires too much skill for the average hobbyist.

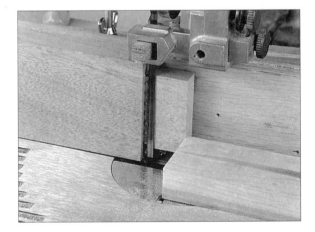

4-73. *Making the second rip cut to define the neck of the tenon. Notice the position of the stop block. The blade should be on the outside of the tenon so that the waste falls away from the fence rather than between the fence and the blade.*

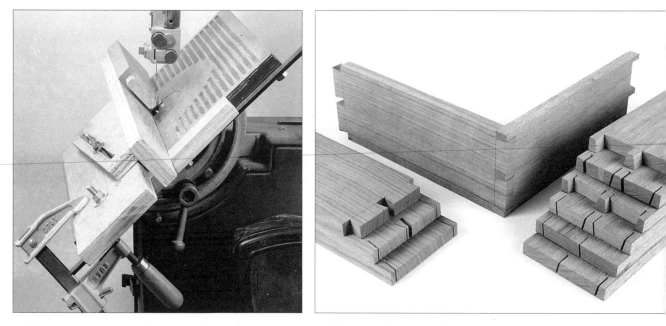

4-74. *Bevel the corners of the tenon by tilting the table to 45 degrees.*

4-75. *Dovetails can be efficiently made with a band saw with the use of a simple jig and spacing blocks. Dovetails made this way allow design flexibility.*

The method of making dovetails described here is an ideal compromise between hand-cut and router-jig methods. It combines the design flexibility of cutting by hand with power-tool accuracy and efficiency (4-75). It allows any tail angle to be used, does not limit stock width or thickness, and is inexpensive and easy to use.

Two problems have to be solved when properly cutting dovetails. First, the cuts for the interlocking pins and tails have to be accurately spaced (4-76). This problem is resolved with the router jig. There are also a number of ways to accurately measure and mark the spaces using the hand method. To facilitate the correct spacing of the cuts, wood spacing blocks are used. When used with a simple guide, the blocks function as the router jig for precisely spacing the angled band-saw cuts.

The second problem is ensuring that the cor-

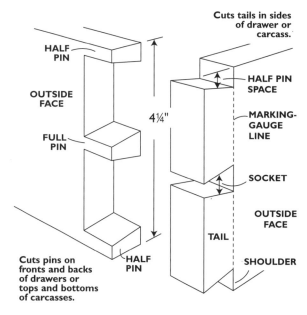

ANATOMY OF A DOVETAIL

4-76. *In order for accurate dovetails to be cut, the angles of the tail and pin pieces must be identical. The spacing between the angles must be the same on each piece.*

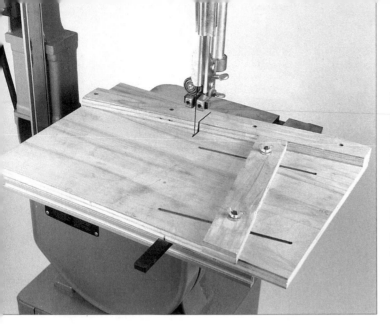

4-77. *The tails are first cut with a plywood jig that holds the workpiece at a 10-degree angle.*

rect angles are cut. When a router is used, the angle of the dovetail bit ensures this. When the wood spacing block is used, a simple angle jig is used to cut the tails and angle the table to cut the pins (4-77 and 4-78).

The angle jig is attached to the plywood base at an 80-degree angle. The blade cuts the angle block. An adjustable fence is attached to the plywood table with toilet bolts. Small aluminum extrusions can be used in this jig. They can be easily placed in dadoes in plywood.

With the technique described here, the width of the pins and tails and their spacing can be varied to achieve practically any aesthetic effect. The blocks that set the spacing are self-centered and will produce perfect-fit-

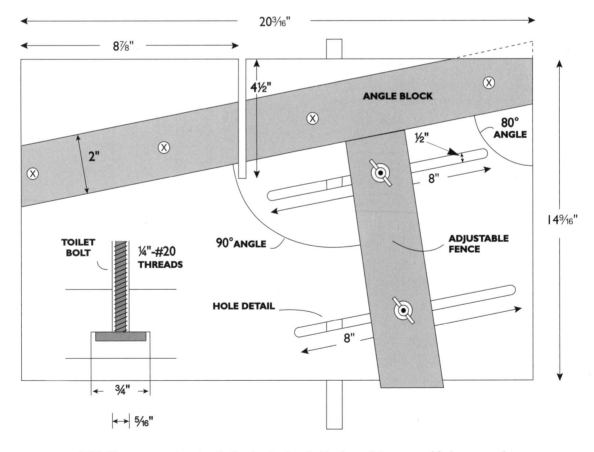

4-78. *The construction details for the jig that holds the tailpiece at a 10-degree angle.*

ting, interchangeable joints. This eliminates the need to mark boards so that individual joints will fit, as is done when hand-dovetailing.

To make dovetails using this technique, begin by preparing the stock accurately. After preparing the stock, score the material with a gauge line. The gauge line prevents tear-out and makes the cut depth easier to see.

The next step consists of making the saw cuts. This consists of spacing the cuts, cutting the tails, and cutting the pins. Each is described below.

Spacing the Cuts

Accurate dovetails can be easily made when wood blocks are used to space the saw cuts. After each cut, remove a spacing block and make a different series of cuts. 4-79 shows the relationship between the blocks and the saw cuts. Each block

spaces the distance from the corner of one tail to the corner of the next tail. The setup on the left of 4-79 shows that the difference between the total width of the blocks (4 inches) and the width of the workpiece (4 ¼ inches) determines the size of the pin and half-pin (¼ inch). As indicated by the setup on the right of 4-79, tail size can be altered by changing block size. When tails of different sizes are used, the design of the joint is affected. Completely different designs can be created by changing the block sizes and the width of the workpiece. When doing this for the first time, use two blocks of the same size. In the example shown in the following illustrations, two 2-inch blocks are used with a workpiece that is 4 ¼ inches wide.

Following are different formulas to use when considering different dovetail designs:

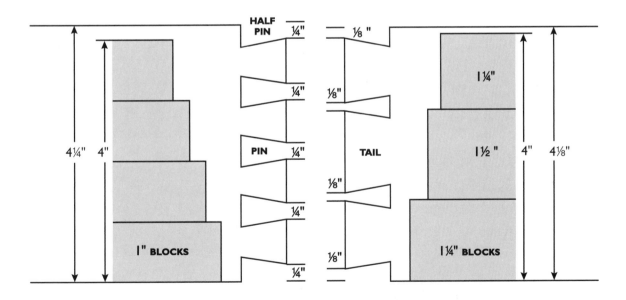

4-79. *Wood blocks space the saw cuts. The relationship between the blocks and the saw cuts is shown here. Each block spaces the distance from the corner of one tail to the corner of the next one. The workpiece on the left is 4¼ inches wide. Each block is 1 inch wide. The difference between the width of the workpiece (4¼ inches) and the width of the blocks (4 inches) is ¼ inch. This is the size of the pins and half pins. Tail size can be changed by changing block size. This allows for variable-pin spacing. The pins shown on the right are ⅛ inch, which is the difference between the 4-inch blocks and the 4⅛-inch board.*

WORKPIECE = total width of blocks and pin size.

PIN SIZE = width of workpiece minus the total block width.

TOTAL BLOCK WIDTH = width of work piece minus the pin size.

Cutting the Tails

Cut the tails first. 4-80 shows the sequence for making the tails. To hold the workpiece and the spacer blocks at the correct angle, the jig described earlier has to be made. Use a piece of plywood with a wood, metal, or plastic strip in the miter slot. First, mark the pin size, which is the difference between the width of the blocks

4-80. The cutting sequence for the tails.

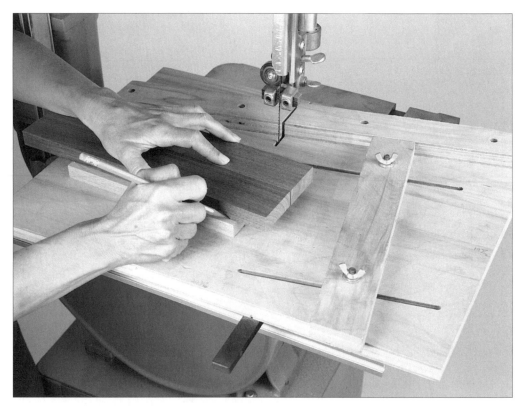

4-81. The blocks are placed on top of the workpiece and a pencil mark is made. This mark represents the difference between the workpiece and the total width of the blocks.

4-82. *The blade is lined up with the pencil mark. The blocks are placed on the jig next to the workpiece and the moveable fence is adjusted.*

4-83. *A cut is made down to the gauge line. Then a stop block and a C-clamp are used to stop the forward movement of the jig. All four corners are cut.*

and the width of the workpiece (4-81). Next, position the blocks and the workpiece on the jig. Place the blocks on the side of the workpiece. The blade and the lead mark should be lined up with each other (4-82).

Make the first cut. Cut to the gauge line and then place a stop on the table so that the jig cannot go forward any farther. Tilt the top wheel rearward far enough so that the blade rides against the thrust bearing. This will prevent the blade from wandering forward over the gauge line. Using a ⅛-inch blade seems to work best for removing the waste.

Next, rotate the board so that all four corners are cut (4-83). Remove a spacing block and repeat the process. 4-84 and 4-85 show the cutting sequence.

The next step is to widen the saw kerf between

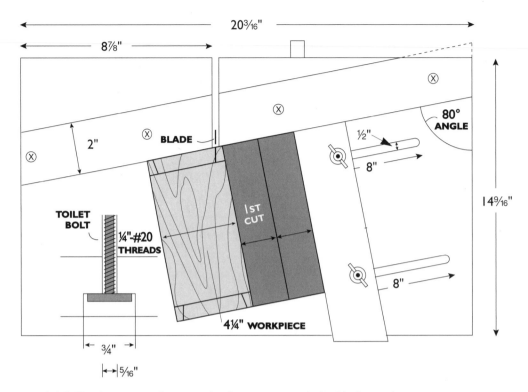

4-84. *The first series of cuts on the four corners with the blocks in place.*

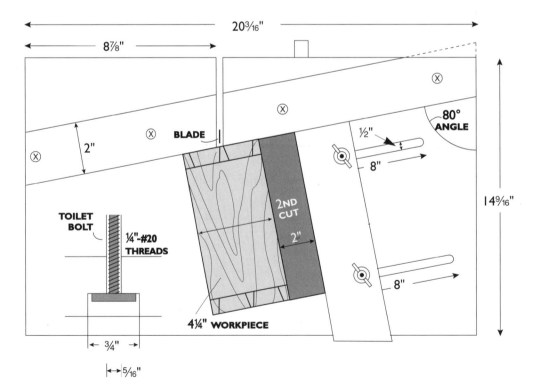

4-85. *The second series of cuts with one of the blocks removed.*

the two inside cuts (4-86). This will expedite waste removal. Some woodworkers may prefer to remove the waste in the traditional way, with a chisel. If this is the case, this step can be disregarded.

The waste can be removed by using the rip fence (refer to 4-99). This is a situation in which a micro-adjuster fence is very handy. Make the waste cut so that the edge of the blade is aligned with the gauge line. Make one cut and then rotate the workpiece to cut the opposite corner. Slip the blade into the wide kerf and

crosscut the waste. Rotate the board 180 degrees to remove the waste from the opposite corner.

Cutting the Pins

Cut the pins after completing the tails. 4-87 shows the cutting sequence. The easiest way to cut them is to tilt the table on the saw and to use the fence to locate the workpiece.

There are two series of cuts involved. The first is done with the workpiece tilted at 10 degrees. The second is done with the table

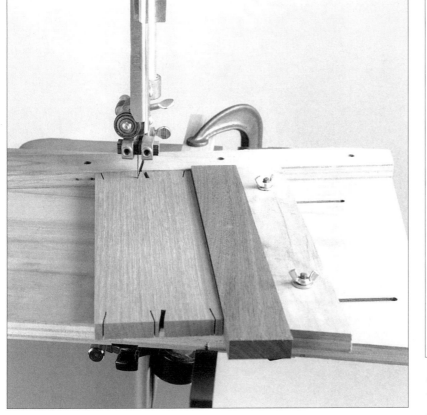

4-86. The workpiece is moved away from the block and the saw kerf is widened until the waste area between the tails is wide enough to accept a 1/8-inch blade.

4-87. The series of cuts required to remove the waste from the pin board. Use two series of 10-degree cuts with the table tilted in opposite directions to make the pins.

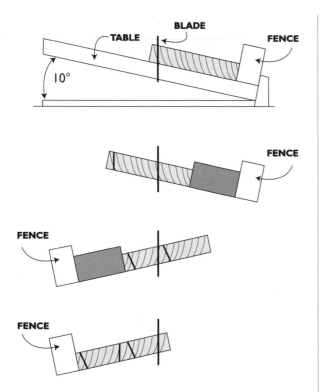

4-88. *End view of the cuts made with the table tilted in opposite directions.*

tilted 10 degrees in the opposite direction (4-88). The tilting can be done with the table or, if the band saw does not tilt 10 degrees in each direction, with a 10-degree angle jig. Position the piece on the jig or place it against a fence. To find the correct starting position, line up the corner of the blade with the outside corner of the tail (4-89 and 4-90). Cut in the waste area.

The cutting sequence for the pins is different than that for the tails. While all four corners of the tails were cut, the opposite corners of the pins will be cut. Start the pin cut on one side and progress to the opposite side (4-91). In this sequence, blocks are added instead of subtracted. A stop should be used to stop the forward progress of the pin board. A square block of wood and a clamp work well.

Make the first series of cuts. Cut the opposite corner instead of all four corners in the manner used to cut the tails. Next, add a block. This will space the next cut. Then repeat the cutting process (4-92).

The second series of pin cuts are made with the table or the jig tilted 10 degrees in the opposite direction (4-93). Place paper shims against the fence for later use when fitting the joint. Align the blade so that it is just short of the tail corner. Use the spacing block for these cuts, as shown in 4-92.

After the first cuts, remove the spacing block and make the next series of cuts (4-94). Make one cut to see if the dovetail fits. With a coping saw,

4-89 (left). *The first step is making pin cuts consists of tilting the table to 10 degrees and lining up the corner of the tail with the blade.*

4-90. Next, the fence is placed into position and locked. The space into which the tail will fit is going to be cut out.

4-92. The second series of pin cuts are made after a spacer block is added. The cuts are made first from one side and then from the opposite side.

4-91. The pin cuts are made first on one side and then the opposite side. Use a stop to set the depth of cut. A large square block of wood works well. It is a good idea to clamp the platform to the saw table.

4-93. The second series of cuts are made with the table angled in the opposite direction. The corner of the tail is lined up with the blade.

4-94. *The single cuts shown here are those made in the second series of cuts. Repeat the previous steps.*

cut off the waste (4-95). Fit the tails to the pin board. If the fit is too tight (which is the objective), make another cut. Take a "hair" off the tails. Make the adjustment with a micro-adjuster or paper shims. If the tails don't fit into the pin board and a micro-adjuster isn't available, do the final fitting by using paper shims against the fence. If the fit is too tight, remove a paper shim (4-96). When enough material has been removed from the second series of cuts, the joint will fit as shown in 4-97. With this cut, the final fit for the entire group of dovetails is being made.

When the tail fits into the pin board, cut off the waste using the rip fence (4-98). The piece may have to be tilted slightly back when the waste cut is being started and cut. 4-99 shows the completed dovetail.

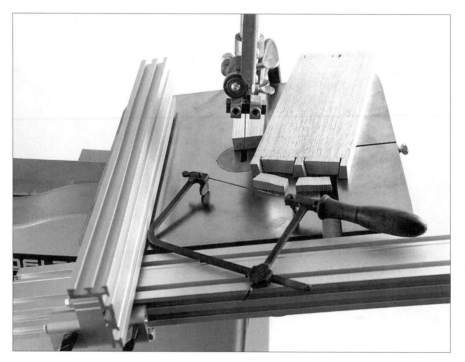

4-95. *The waste is removed with a coping saw and then the pins are fitted to the tail board.*

4-96. *The cut is then expanded. The wide cut allows for easy entry of a 1/8-inch blade, so the waste can be crosscut. If the joint is too tight, an adjustment can be made by adding paper shims against the fence to trim a "hair" off the pin board.*

4-97. *Make adjustments with paper shims until the pins and tails fit together.*

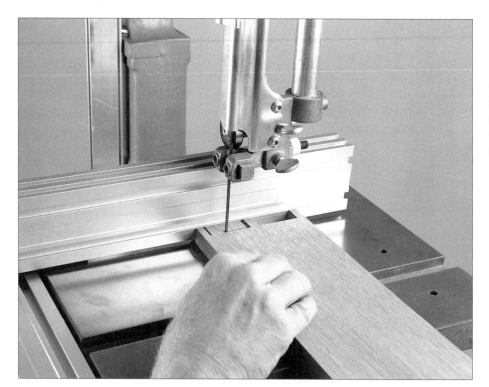

4-98. *The area between the pins is removed by crosscutting the waste with the pin board against the fence.*

4-99. *The completed tails and pins. All of the work was done with the band saw.*

5 Patterns and Templates

Patterns

The usual practice when using a band saw is to trace an outline of the shape on the workpiece with a pencil, and to create this shape by cutting just outside the pencil line. For this reason, a drawing of the desired shape is placed on top of the workpiece. This is the pattern. A pattern can be drawn directly onto the workpiece or it can be drawn or copied onto a piece of paper which is then attached to the workpiece. The paper can be taped in place or attached with an adhesive such as rubber cement.

The advantage of using a pattern is that it shows exactly what the project will look like.

SOURCES OF PATTERNS

Patterns can be found in woodworking magazines and books. They can also be ordered from a variety of sources such as mail-order companies. They can be used exactly as shown or modified slightly.

Patterns can also be made. A person with good drawing skills can draw the pattern to scale and then revise the drawing as needed. Another approach when repairing or replacing a part from a piece of furniture is to trace the part onto a piece of paper or glue the broken pieces back together to form a pattern.

CHANGING THE SIZES OF PATTERNS

There are times when the size of a pattern has to be enlarged or reduced. The easiest way to do this is to use a photocopier. New photocopiers can expand or shrink patterns in one-percent increments.

Another way to change the size of a pattern is to use a pantograph. This is a mechanical device that is used to change the scale of the drawing (5–1). It is very easy to use. The enlargement or reduction

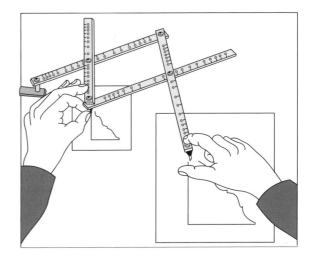

5-1. A pantograph is a mechanical device that is used to enlarge or reduce a drawing. The design is drawn on paper (shown on the left). Then the follower point is guided along the original design, while the pencil point (shown on the right) automatically recreates the outline in its exact size. (Drawing courtesy of Lee Valley Tools, L.T.D., Ottawa, Canada.)

is drawn directly onto the workpiece or onto a piece of paper. The follower point is guided along the original design, while the pencil point automatically recreates the outline in its exact proportions in a desired size.

There is a third way to change the size of patterns that applies to those offered in magazines and books, which are often printed in a reduced size and have to be transferred to the workpiece. The patterns are generally drawn on a grid, which helps to break the pattern down into small, easily transferred components.

Let's take as an example the Shaker hanging shelf shown in 5-2. In the plan for this hanging shelf (5-3), the front and side views of the project are of a reduced size. The curved shapes for the front and the side are covered with a grid. When the grid is enlarged to the point that each square is 1-inch square, the pattern is the correct size.

The pattern is enlarged by making a grid on a piece of paper or using a sheet of graph paper (which already has grids). With the intersecting lines used as a reference, the pattern is transferred using corresponding dots (5-4). It may be helpful to number the lines in both directions on both the large and small patterns. Use a French curve, profile gauge, or curved rules to connect the dots to form the lines of the desired pattern.

DETERMINING WHICH TYPE OF PATTERN TO USE

There are several types of patterns that are useful in different situations. They are full, half, quarter, double, and compound-sawing patterns. Each is discussed below.

Full-Pattern   A full-pattern, as its name indicates, contains the entire pattern. It is used when the shape of the object is not symmetrical, that is, its proportions are not balanced. The side profile for the Shaker hanging shelf that is shown in 5-3 is a full-pattern.

Half-Pattern   A half-pattern is only half of the shape. When the object is symmetrical, a half pattern is the best pattern to use. The same half-pattern can be used for both sides of an object by drawing one side and then flipping the pattern over. An example of when a half-pattern will be well-used is the front profile for the Shaker hanging shelf. Because both sides of the pattern are

5-2. The Shakers made a large number of hanging shelves. These shelves were suspended from a peg by a leather string. They could also be attached directly to the wall. They are examples of projects that may require some resawing because some of the material is only ¼ inch thick. Shaker shelves are good projects on which to use pattern-sawing, which ensures that both sides of the piece are exactly the same shape. Refer to Pattern-Sawing on pages 127 and 128 for more information.

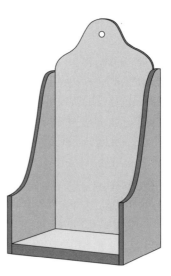

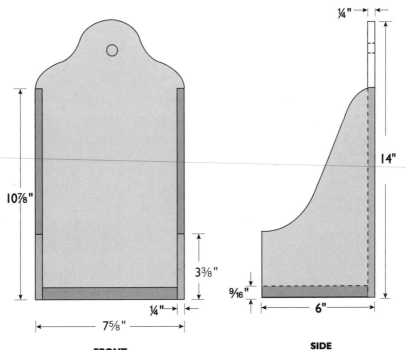

FRONT

¼"

14"

9/16"

6"

SIDE

10⅞"

3⅜"

¼"

7⅝"

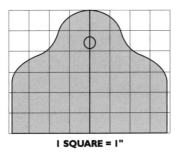

I SQUARE = I"

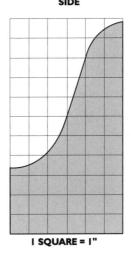

I SQUARE = I"

5-3. *Plans for the Shaker hanging shelf shown in 5-2.*

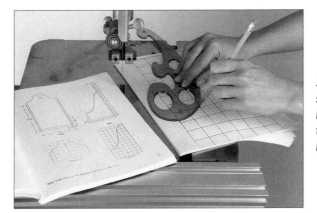

5-4. *Because both sides of the front shelf profile are the same, a half-pattern is drawn. One side is drawn first. Then the pattern is flipped, and the other half is drawn.*

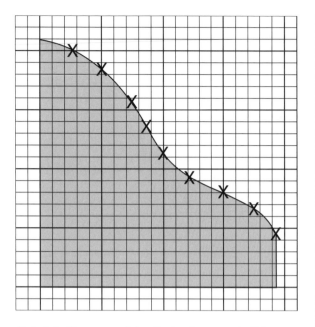

5-5. *A half-pattern of the Shaker hanging shelf front.*

symmetrical, only half of the pattern is drawn on the 1-inch grid graph paper (5-5).

Quarter-Pattern When the object has four corners that are the same, such as in the case of an oval shape, a quarter-pattern is useful (5-6). The pattern is flipped left-to-right, and then top-to-bottom.

Double-Pattern When the object has the same profile from two adjacent sides, the pattern can be used twice.

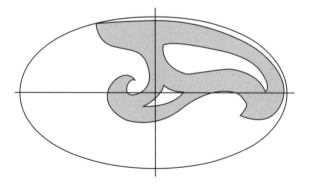

5-6. *Using a quarter-pattern to lay out an oval shape. A French curve is being used for the layout.*

An example of this is the pattern for a cabriole leg. See Making Cabriole Legs on pages 94 and 95.

Compound-Sawn Pattern A compound-sawn pattern is a pattern that is sawn from two adjacent sides. In such situations, two series of cuts are needed to release the workpiece.

The boat profile in 5-7 is an example of a situation in which compound-sawing should be used. After sawing the pattern on one side, re-attach the waste pieces that contain the pattern to use on the adjacent side of the workpiece so that the pattern can be cut again. Use nails, hot-melt glue, or tape to reattach the separated pieces. Plan ahead. This makes it easier to make the cuts. For example, it is easier to make the last series of cuts on the boat profile when it is lying flat rather than on its side.

PATTERN-USING GUIDELINES

Follow these guidelines when laying out and cutting patterns:

1. If planning multiple pieces, place the patterns as close together as possible to avoid wasting material.

2. Mark the waste area of a pattern. Do this because when cutting it is possible to get confused as to which part is the waste and which is the workpiece. A red crayon makes a good marker.

3. When laying out the pattern on the workpiece, it is essential that the direction of the wood grain be considered. The pattern should be used in such a way that maximum grain strength is achieved. This is especially important when thin sections are used.

4. Use plywood instead of solid wood if there is a weakness in the wood grain no matter which direction the grain follows, and/or if the design has a sharp curve.

5-7. *Compound-sawing is a technique in which a pattern is cut from two adjacent sides. The second cut or series of cuts is made with the piece resting on its widest surface. Here the pattern for a boat model is being compound-sawn.*

Templates

Paper patterns are not durable. If patterns will be used often, it is advisable to make the patterns out of durable material such as Masonite (a type of fiberboard), plywood, or plastic. These patterns are known as templates. The template is used to trace the pattern directly onto the workpiece.

Templates are useful on some large workpieces where part of the pattern can be drawn on opposite sides of the workpiece (5-8). Clear-plastic templates are especially useful because the grain of the wood can be seen through the template.

PATTERN-SAWING

Pattern-sawing is a technique used to make multiple identical pieces. A solid template is attached to the workpiece. This technique works best if the pattern is made of plywood, because plywood, unlike solid wood, is stable (does not shrink or expand). The waste material is then removed with the band-saw blade near the pattern, but not touching it. The rest of the waste is removed with a router bit. This technique is particularly useful for projects that have a number of pieces with multiple curves that are exactly the same size.

Following are the step-by-step techniques for pattern-sawing:

1. Clamp a rub block to the saw table (5-9). The rub block should have a curved end with a notch in it. The notch fits over the blade, extending past it about ¹⁄₁₆ inch. Cut out the workpiece so that the workpiece can slide underneath it.

2. Next, tape the plywood pattern to the workpiece with double-faced tape. The pattern will contact the rub block during the cut (5-10).

3. Because the blade is about ¹⁄₁₆ inch short of the pattern, the workpiece extends past the pattern about ¹⁄₁₆ inch (5-11). Therefore, the ¹⁄₁₆-inch waste has to be trimmed away using a router table and a "flush-cutting" router bit (5-12). A flush-cutting router bit is a bit with a bearing on top of it. The bearing rubs against the pattern as the bit trims the waste. The finish is smooth and requires little sanding.

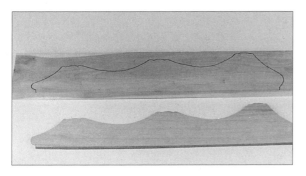

5-8. *A plywood template used to make the design for cherry shelf sides.*

Refer to Pattern-Sanding Jigs, Pattern-Sawing-and-Sanding Jigs, and Pattern-Routing Jigs on pages 140 to 143 for additional related information. Also refer to Determining Blade Width Using a Radius Chart on page 35 for information on determining blade width when cutting patterns.

PATTERN-SAWING

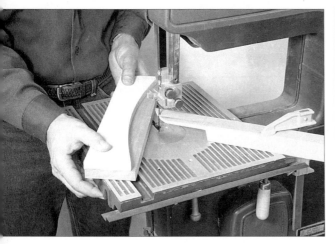

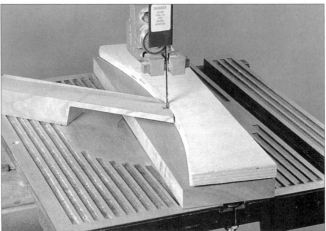

5-9. *The rub block is clamped to the table. The notch in the rub block fits over the blade and protrudes past it about ³⁄₁₆ inch. Double-faced tape is used to attach the template to the workpiece. The template is pressed firmly onto the tape. Do not use too much of the tape or it will be difficult to remove the template.*

5-10. *The cut is begun with the template touching the rub block. As the cutting continues, slight pressure is used to keep the template against the rub block.*

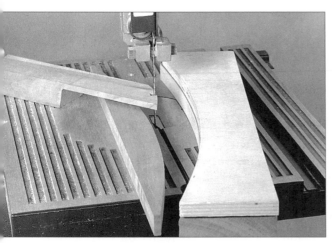

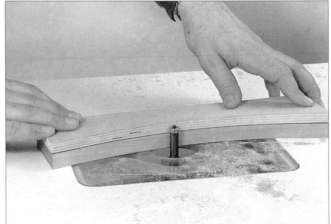

5-11. *The completed cut. The workpiece should extend ³⁄₁₆ inch past the pattern.*

5-12. *While the template is still attached to the pattern, the waste can be trimmed off with a router. The router bit being used for this operation is a flush-cutting bit. The bearing on top of the bit rides against the pattern.*

6 Making and Using Jigs and Fixtures

CHAPTER

The terms jig and fixture refer to store-bought or user-made accessories that serve as aids in the workshop. A fixture is a device that positions or holds the work. A jig positions or holds the work and also guides the tool.

The following sections in this chapter contain information on making and using a variety of jigs and fixtures to perform many different tasks with the band saw. They include a standard V-block fixture, a bevel-cutting fixture, a rip fence, and jigs used to cut circles and tapers, to saw, rout, and sand patterns, to make curved moldings, and to sandwich the workpiece between two identical patterns. Most of them are simple to make, and will help speed up the job and make it more accurate.

V-Block Fixture

The standard V-block is a simple fixture that gets clamped to the rip fence (6-1). Although it performs the same task as can be accomplished when the table is tilted, it does it faster. Also, a V-block is often easier to adjust, particularly when the corners are removed from tenons that will be fit into rounded router-made mortises. Refer to Making Mortise-and-Tenon Joints on pages 108-110 for more information.

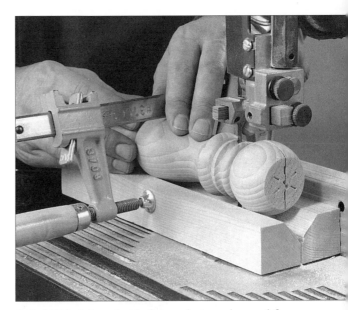

6-1. A V-block is a simple fixture that can be used for a variety of purposes, including cutting round stock.

Bevel-Cutting Fixture

Illus. 6-2 and 6-3 show a four-foot-long user-made fixture which supports a large piece of wood as it is cut on an angle. Its main purpose is to support the work on each side of the table. If the band-saw's table-tilting capacity were used instead of this fixture, the board would be cut at the correct angle, but the long workpiece would not be properly supported. The opposite side of

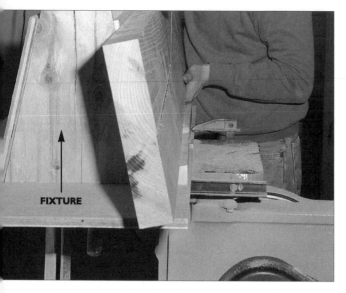

6-2. *This bevel-cutting fixture is being used to rip a long piece of 3 x 12 oak. It is 4 feet long and extends past the saw table on each end to support the work. It is an example of a single-purpose fixture.*

6-3. *The bevel-cutting fixture being used to make a cut.*

the fixture has the same angle, but it also has a curved support on the bottom for making a beveled cut on a curved workpiece (6-4 to 6-6). 6-7 shows the construction details for making this fixture.

6-4 to 6-6. *Cutting a curved piece with a bevel-cutting fixture. Here the jig holds the curved piece at the correct angle.*

6-5. *During the cut, the curved bottom of the workpiece slides along the curved bottom of the fixture.*

6-6. *A bevel cut on the curved piece that was made with the fixture.*

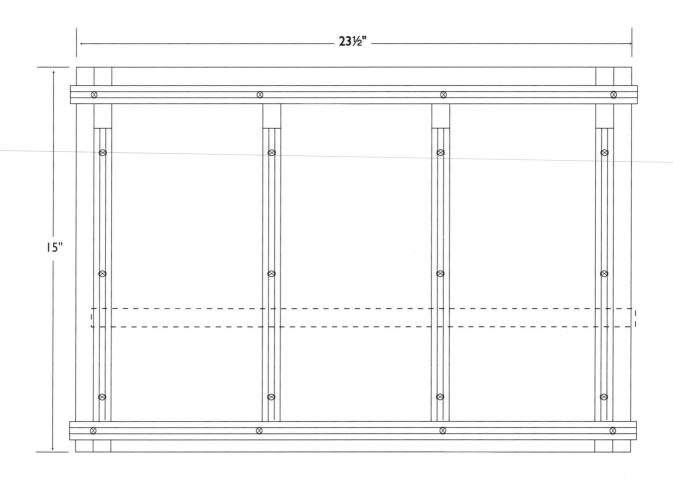

6-7. *Construction details for the bevel-cutting fixture.*

Rip Fences

The rip fence is an optional piece of equipment that can be bought for most band saws. Some of the older saws, however, do not have rip fences available. A rip fence for ripping or resawing can be made. It consists of two pieces of plywood secured at a 90-degree angle. The fence is clamped to the front and back of the table. (This type of rip fence is described and illustrated in Using a Rip Fence to Cut Curved Multiple Pieces on pages 84 and 85.)

At times, it is useful to be able to move the fence a fraction of an inch. 6-8 to 6-13 show a user-made rip fence that has this microadjusting ability. It has two tapered surfaces that slide against each other. This jig has a one-to-six ratio, which is about 80 degrees. This means that if the fence is moved forward one inch, it will move toward the blade one-sixth of an inch. A jig with a one-to-eight ratio can also be built. This would move the jig sideways one-eighth of an inch for each inch of forward movement.

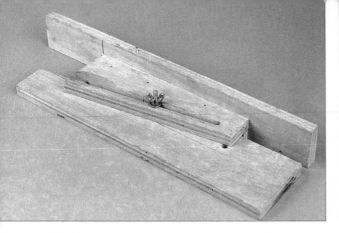
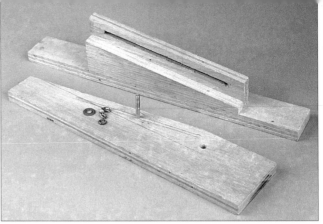

6-8. This microadjusting rip fence is made from scrap plywood.

6-9. Each piece of the fence has an angled side. To change the fence position, move it forward or rearward.

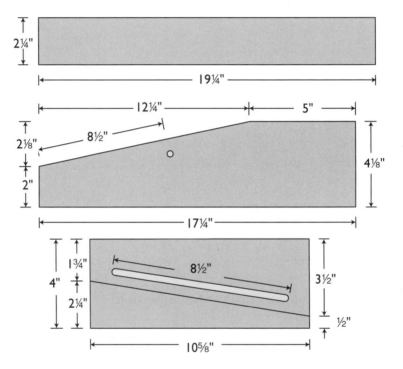

2¼"

19¼"

12¼"

5"

2⅛"

8½"

2"

4⅛"

17¼"

4"

1¾"

2¼"

8½"

3½"

½"

10⅝"

6-10. Construction details for the micro-adjusting rip fence.

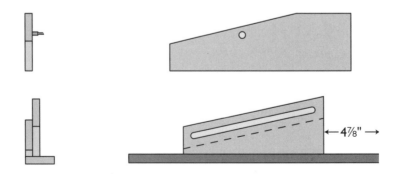

4⅞"

6-11. Side view of the jig.

6-12. *The fence can be adjusted for the correct cutting angles. To do this, add a bottom piece with sandpaper on top of it. Use a carriage bolt to attach the bottom piece to the top one.*

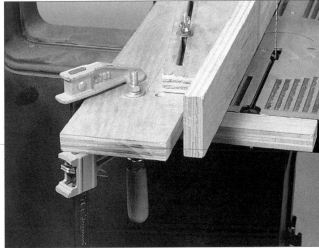

6-13. *The fence is attached to the table with a clamp.*

Jigs for Circular Work

Many projects require either complete circles or a portion of a circle. Although it is possible to cut a circle freehand, this is not the most accurate way. The most accurate way would be to use a circle-cutting jig.

The basic idea involved in using a circle-cutting jig is to locate a rotation point a certain distance from the blade. The rotation point is held in place by the jig. As the workpiece rotates on the point, the circle is cut. The work is rotated around the point just as a compass rotates around a central point. The distance between the point and the blade determines the radius of the circle.

Several types of circle-cutting jigs can be used. They include the full-circle-cutting jig, half-circle jigs, and quarter-circle jigs. In addition, off-center rotation points can be used with these jigs. Each is described below.

FULL-CIRCLE-CUTTING JIGS

Full-circle-cutting jigs are commercially available or can be user-made. Both types work the same way. Commercial jigs are usually adjustable, so that the radius of the circle can be easily changed. The rotation point can be either above or below the workpiece. A rotation point below the workpiece has some advantages, especially if the jig is used to cut half- and quarter-circles.

6-14 and 6-15 show a user-made plywood jig with a rotation point located on a pencil line that is even with the front of the blade. The rotation point is simply a sharpened nail. The jig consists of a solid piece of wood that fits in the miter slot. It is attached to the bottom of the plywood platform. The jig slides in the miter slot. Its forward motion is stopped by a piece of wood clamped to the wooden miter bar (6-16). It is important that the rotation point is even with the front of the blade.

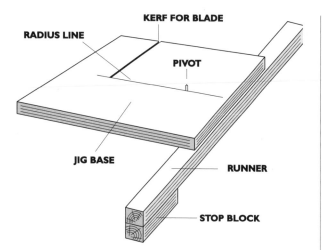

6-14. *A user-made plywood full-circle-cutting jig. The jig slides in the miter slot. A stop block at the end of the miter slot is adjustable. A stop block is made by clamping a piece of scrap wood to the miter-guide piece. It should stop the jig when the rotation point is even with the front of the saw blade.*

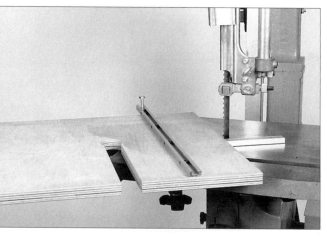

6-15. *The full-circle-cutting jig.*

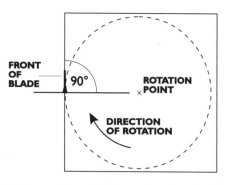

6-16. *The rotation point has to be aligned with the front of the blade.*

The full-circle-cutting jig is easy to make. Do the following:

1. Cut two pieces of wood for the jig. One should be a piece of plywood about 16 inches square. The other should be a piece of solid wood the size of the miter slot.

2. Cut about two inches off the end of the plywood piece. This will later be clamped to the strip and used as a stop.

3. Nail the plywood and solid-wood pieces together.

4. After the pieces are nailed together, advance the piece of plywood into the blade until it is cut halfway across.

5. Turn off the saw and make a mark 90 degrees to the saw cut (6-17). The rotation point is located on this pencil line.

6. Adjust the stop so that the front tip of the tooth touches the pencil line. Use a nail or screw as the rotation point. The radius of the circle is the distance between the blade and the rotation point.

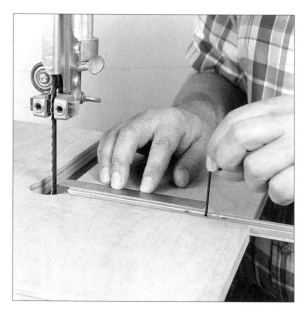

6-17. *Making a mark 90 degrees to the saw cut.*

To use the jig, do the following:

1. Puncture a small hole into the center of the workpiece (6-18) and mount the workpiece onto the point.

2. Move the jig and the workpiece into the blade until the stop touches the table (6-19).

3. Slowly rotate the workpiece on the point until the circle is completed (6-20).

If the table is angled, the circle that is cut will be wider at the top than at the bottom. This is useful when thick circles are being cut to be used for bowl blanks. If this jig is used, more accurate bowl blanks will be made.

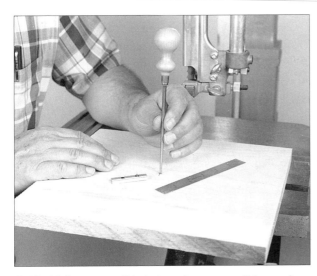

6-18. *Making a small hole into the center of the work-piece.*

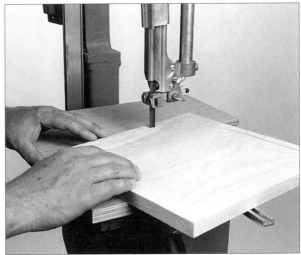

6-19. *When using the bottom pivot point, move the jig and workpiece forward to create a straight line. When the rotation point is even with the front of the saw blade, rotate the work to create the circle. The adjustable stop block clamped to the miter-slot runner should contact the table as the front of the blade touches the radius line.*

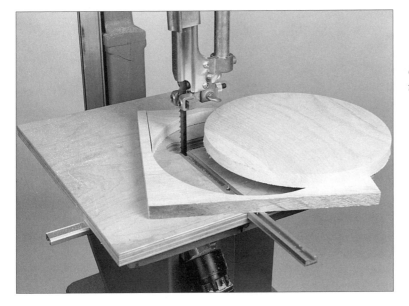

6-20. *Slowly rotate the workpiece on the point until the circle is completed.*

HALF-CIRCLE JIGS

Many projects require partial circles. User-made jigs prove helpful in cutting partial circles. There are three methods for cutting partial circles with a jig. The first consists of advancing the jig and the workpiece into the blade. An easier method consists of clamping the jig to the table and rotating only the workpiece into the blade.

A third way of cutting partial circles is to use a jig that holds the workpiece in conjunction with a full-circle-cutting jig. This jig will rest on top of the full-circle-cutting jig. The jig and the workpiece are rotated together.

The half-circle jig is a piece of plywood with a rotation point on the bottom of it (6-21 and 6-22). Two plywood sides are added to stabilize the workpiece. A clamp is used to hold the workpiece in place during the saw cut.

To make a half-circle jig, do the following:

1. Cut a piece of plywood that is the diameter of the circle.

2. Make a hole for the rotation point. The hole should be half the width of the plywood (which is the radius of the circle).

3. Using the rotation point, make the half-circle cut in the plywood (6-23).

4. Attach the two sides to the plywood base (6-24 and 6-25). This will keep the workpieces stable during the cut. A quick-action clamp can also be used to secure the workpiece to the jig.

6-21. The half-circle jig consists of a piece of plywood with strips of plywood nailed to its sides. An adjustable clamp is used to hold the workpiece during the saw cut.

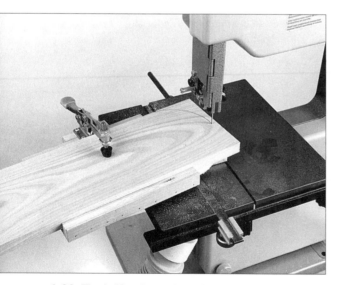

6-22. The half-circle jig shown lying on the full-circle-cutting jig, which is a piece of plywood. The full-circle-cutting jig, a commercial jig that is manufactured by INCA, is not shown here. The cut shown here is half-completed.

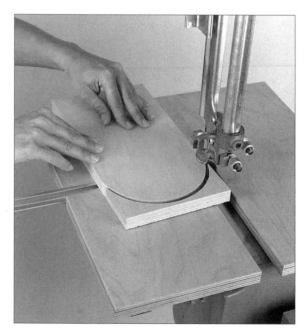

6-23. Making the half-circle cut in the plywood.

6-24. *The plywood base and the pieces that are attached to its sides*

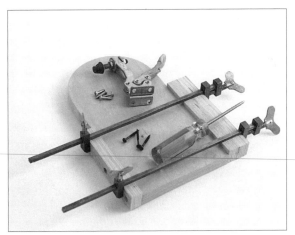

6-25. *The side pieces glued and clamped to the plywood base.*

QUARTER-CIRCLE JIGS

Quarter-circle jigs are used to make "radius" cuts. A "radius" cut is a cut made in the corner of the workpiece, which forms a quarter-circle (6-26).

Quarter-circle jigs consist of two strips of wood attached to each side of a complete piece (6-27 and 6-28). To make one, do the following:

1. Determine the radius of the partial circle.
2. Measure the distance from each edge of the workpiece to the rotation point.

6-26. *A quarter-circle cut is usually referred to as a radius cut.*

6-27. *A quarter-circle jig is made by adding a wood strip to each side. The workpiece is held in the corner of the jig and the cut is made. The cut can be made without the need to measure, mark, or make a hole.*

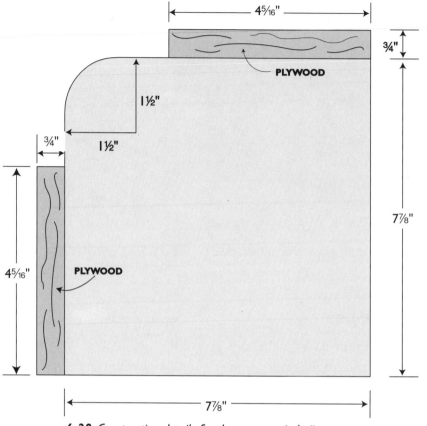

6-28. Construction details for the quarter-circle jig.

3. Locate the rotation point, and cut the corner off.

4. Add two pieces of wood to the side.

5. Rotate the workpiece and the jig into the blade.

6. Cut the corner. A puncture hole does not have to be made.

To make radius cuts, mark the centerpoint of the circle by making two equal measurements, one from each edge. Use an awl to mark the point and to make a hole. Move the jig nail or point to a location that is the proper distance from the blade. This distance is the same measurement as the radius. Then place the workpiece hole over the jig point and make the cut (6-29).

6-29. The work is placed on the quarter-circle-cutting jig point and the piece is rotated into the saw blade, thus making a quarter-circle.

CORNER ROTATION POINT

Off-center rotation points can be used with the circle-cutting jigs just described to cut interesting designs for projects easily and accurately. One type of off-center rotation point, called a corner rotation point, is used to remove a quarter-circle of waste.

A corner rotation point was used to make the cuts for the Shaker step stool in 6-30. This jig consists of an aluminum extrusion that is dadoed into a piece of plywood (6-31). The rotation point slides in the extrusion and is locked in place with an Allen key. In this case, the rotation point is located between the column and the blade (6-32 and 6-33).

The actual half-circle-making technique used on the Shaker step stool consisted of cutting the quarter-circles that made the step stool before gluing them together. Because the rotation point was located on that part of the workpiece that would be waste material, a small hole was drilled into the corner of the workpiece and the workpiece was nailed to the jig.

USING A CORNER ROTATION POINT

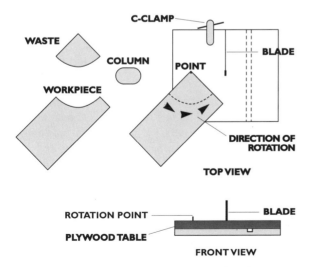

6-30. *This Shaker table features half-circles as a design element.*

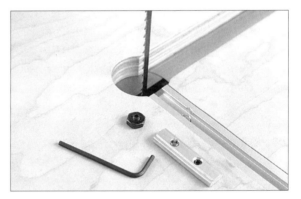

6-31. *This corner rotation point consists of an aluminum extension dadoed into a piece of plywood. The point slides into the extrusion and is locked in place with an Allen key.*

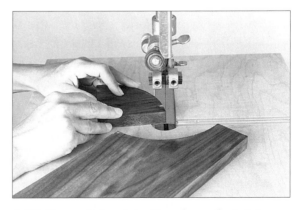

6-32. *The corner rotation point is clamped to the saw table. Its corner is positioned between the blade and the column, and the workpiece is rotated into the blade.*

6-33. *The workpiece is positioned over the point, which is located between the blade and the column. With this arrangement, the workpiece doesn't rotate into the column. The completed cut is shown here.*

Taper-Cutting Jigs

There are three types of jigs used to cut tapers, which are angled cuts made along the grain of the workpiece. As shown in 4-63 on page 106, they are fixed-angle jigs, step jigs, and adjustable taper jigs. The fixed-angle jig, the simplest of the three to make, is an angled piece of wood with a brass screw in one end which pushes the workpiece through the end. The step jig has three notches or steps, and is used to make a taper on one side, opposite sides, or adjacent sides of the workpiece. The adjustable taper jig, which has a hinge on one end and a locking mechanism on the opposite, can be adjusted to the desired angle.

Refer to Cutting Tapers on pages 105 to 107 for information on making and using fixed-angle, step, and adjustable taper jigs.

Pattern-Sanding Jigs

Pattern-sanding is the technique of using a sanding drum on a drill press to smooth patterns. It is an alternative to pattern-routing, which is described in the following section. Pattern-routing and pattern-sanding are used to smooth the pattern after it has been sawn.

Almost any type of pattern can be pattern-sanded, but this technique works best on curves that would create tear-out from a router bit. The pattern-sanding jig is useful to build when multiple identical pieces have to be made, because it speeds up the work.

The Shaker table in 6-34 is an example of a project in which pattern-sanding is worthwhile. The two-sided jig in 6-35 will hold two workpieces at one time, shaping the concave side on one and the convex side of the other. The pattern is below the workpiece.

6-34. This three-legged round table is typical of many tables designed by the Shakers. This type of table is the simplest to make and doesn't require the turning skills needed for some of the more-complex tables. The table-top is cut with a band saw and a circle-cutting jig or a router. The post is turned, and the three legs are dovetailed into the post.

6-35. This jig is designed to hold two table legs so that the inside and outside of the legs can both be sanded at the same time. The sander has a solid phenolic disc on its bottom which does not rotate and functions like a flush-trim bit. It is handy for situations like this, when the grain is not straight.

A sanding drum is used on a drill press with a phenolic follower on its bottom. It works like a flush-trim router bit, although a starting pin is not needed (6-36).

6-36. *Using the sander in a drill press.*

Pattern-Sawing-and-Sanding Jigs

Pattern-sawing and -sanding techniques can be combined to shape any number of curved pieces. Let's take the example of the rail used on a chair back. In this instance, a simple curved board is used to shape a curve part. This involves the use of the band saw and a drill press.

Here is how to make the rail of a chair back using pattern-sawing and -sanding: Make a curved board on the band saw with the desired full-sized pattern on one side of the board. Sand or plane the board smooth. The back of the pattern should be flat, so that it can be attached to the blank. Prepare the stock and make the tenons while the wood is square.

Next, attach a spacer block to the band-saw fence. This spacer block should be about 3 inches square. It will serve as a follower. Then attach the pattern to the workpiece with double-sided carpet tape. Saw the workpiece by running the curved face of the pattern against the support block. This cut doesn't make the full curve. It

6-38 (right). *The curved block and the workpiece are then passed through a disc sander. The follower board is clamped to the table. After each pass, the follower board can be advanced forward slightly.*

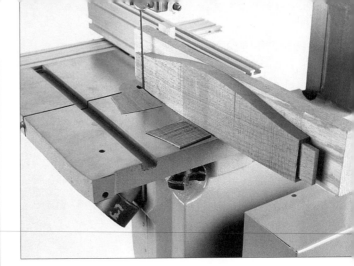

6-37. *The chair slat is attached to the straight side of the curved block with double-faced tape. A two-inch block is attached to the rip fence with double-faced tape. The middle of the rip-fence block should be aligned with the saw blade. The workpiece is fed into the blade, and a tapered waste piece is removed.*

just removes the thick part of the waste on each end of the board (6-37).

Next, take the workpiece and the curved pattern board to the disc sander. Again, make a follower board with a slight angle on it. Clamp the follower board to the sander table. The follower board must be precisely located on the table, square to the disc sander and a set distance away from it.

Now, pass the assembled pattern and workpiece between the disc and the follower board (6-38). If the proper technique and fine sandpaper are used, the finish will be quite good. This completes the outside of the curve except for scraping

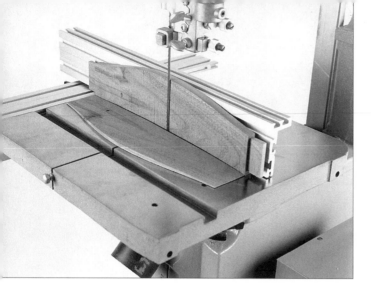

6-39. *Making the inside curve. Notice that this curve is thicker in the middle, and that the outside curve is thinner than it. The inside curve can be sanded with a sanding drum on the drill press, as shown in 6-40. The concave side rests against the fence as the waste is removed.*

6-40. *The sanding drum on the drill press is used to finish the concave side. A micro-adjuster on this drill press allows multiple passes to be adjusted in small increments*

and sanding. A woodworker skillful with a hand plane can skip this sanding method and smooth the curve with a sharp plane.

Next, remove the part from the curved pattern board. Use the completed outside curve as the pattern for making the inside curve on the band saw (6-39). Then feed the workpiece through the band saw with the outside of the curve bearing against the fence. The saw will follow this curve, creating a parallel inside surface.

The inside curve is sanded with the sanding drum on the drill press, with the outside of the workpiece being used as a template. The distance between the sanding drum and the drill-press fence should be set to the final thickness of the part. Feed the part past the drum, keeping the outside of the curve against the fence. Feed against the rotation of the drum (6-40). A woodworker skilled with hand tools can clean up the concave side with a spokeshave and a scraper.

Pattern-Routing Jigs

Pattern-routing is used in conjunction with pattern-sawing. In pattern-sawing, the shape is

rough-cut on the band saw. Pattern-routing is the technique of smoothing the shape by attaching a template to the workpiece and using a flush-trim router bit to remove the waste (6-41 and 6-42).

One way to attach the template to the top of the workpiece is with double-faced tape. When making multiple pieces, it is easier to make a pattern out of ½-inch plywood and clamp the workpiece to it. The pattern serves as the jig.

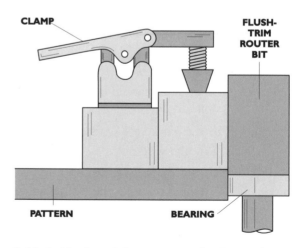

6-41. *A side view of the pattern-routing jigs used to make legs. The workpiece is clamped to the pattern, which contacts the bearing.*

6-42. *This pattern-routing jig is being used to cut the back of a chair leg. Use the starter pin in the router table for pattern-routing operations.*

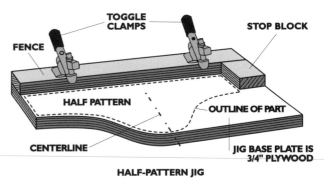

6-43. *A half-pattern jig holds the workpiece while half of the shape is being routed. This is done by releasing the clamps, turning the workpiece over and end for end, and cutting the second part of the curve.*

WITH-THE-GRAIN PATTERN-ROUTING JIGS

When pattern-routing curved work, the wood grain poses a problem that isn't a factor when the wood is being sawed. Routing against the grain almost always causes tear-out. Usually, half of the pattern is cut with the grain, and the other half against the grain.

A simple and very effective way to avoid tear-out is to change the feed direction of the workpiece partway along the curve, so that routing is always done with the grain. This means rotating the workpiece 180 degrees and then feeding it from the opposite side.

There are two types of pattern-routing jigs that allow the direction of the workpiece to be changed: half-pattern jigs and sandwich jigs. Each has advantages. Both are generally used on the router table. They are discussed in the following section.

A third jig used to make curve molding is included here because it is used to cut with and against the grain.

Half-Pattern Jigs

Half-pattern jigs should be used to rout a symmetrical part (6-43). Because the entire profile isn't being routed all at once, there is no need to make a pattern for the entire shape.

Cut out the curve of the pattern and then sand it to shape. It should extend past each side of the workpiece. Use fences and stop blocks to position the workpiece on the patterns. Add clamps. Rough-cut the shape on the band saw (6-44).

The next step involves shaping the pattern on a router table with a hand-held router. Using a starter pin, start the cut on the flat part of the jig with the grain. When half of the shape is cut, flip the workpiece over and cut the waste off the other half. Remember to cut the tenons first.

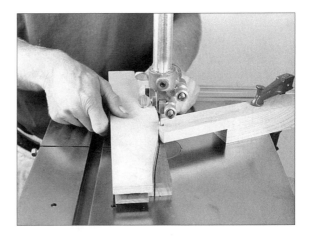

6-44. *Using a half-pattern jig to rough-cut a symmetrical part.*

Sandwich Jigs

A sandwich jig holds the workpiece between two identical patterns (6-45). Tear-out can be avoided by flipping the entire assembly over whenever the grain changes direction (6-46). A jig like this is time-consuming to make but is particularly helpful when multiple pieces with changing grain are being made for projects like the Shaker table leg

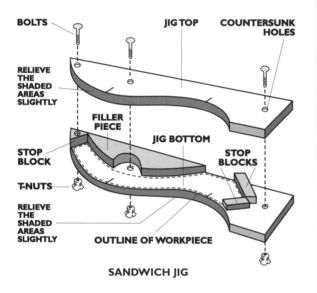

6-45. *The sandwich jig holds the work between the identical patterns.*

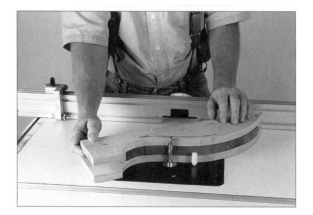

6-46. *A sandwich jig permits the woodworker to cut with the grain by flipping the assembly when the wood grain changes directions. The white plastic peg is a starting pin, which helps in starting and stopping the cut.*

6-47. *The flowing curves on this table are a typical Shaker design element. The outside of the three legs has a double curve. A sandwich jig is useful for efficiently making the legs identical.*

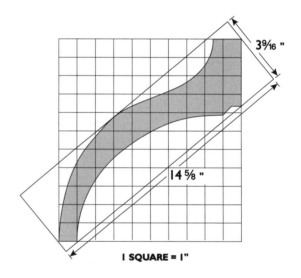

6-48. *Leg detail for the Shaker table shown in 6-47.*

shown in 6-47 and 6-48. Marks on the jig locate the points at which the direction is changed. Bolts and T-nuts should be used as clamps.

To make a sandwich jig, first make up two identical patterns. Then accurately cut a workpiece blank to size and trace its outline on one of the patterns. Locate the bolt positions on this pattern, avoiding the area where the workpiece will be. Two or three bolts are usually enough.

As with the other pattern-routing jigs, always

use a starter pin when using the jig on the router table. To avoid cutting into the jig accidentally with the router bit, a straight router bit that is fit into a guide bushing is used instead of a flush-trim router bit. The bottom pattern rubs against the guide bushing and trims the waste off the workpiece (6-49 and 6-50). The pattern is slightly smaller than the workpiece.

Spiral cutters can be used instead of the straight router bit. They produce a very smooth surface.

Jigs for Making Curved Molding

Curved moldings are often used as decorative elements. For example, clocks and highboy chest often have sweeping curved molding atop their bonnets (6-51). The traditional way of making this molding is to carve it with chisels and gouges, which is very slow and tedious. A much quicker way is to use pattern-sawing and pattern-routing techniques. Jigs can be used to make carved moldings utilizing these techniques (6-52).

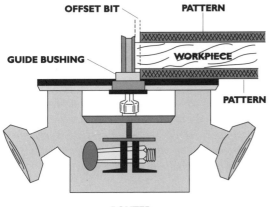

6-49. *The patterns rub against the guide bushing, which prevents the straight bit from contacting and cutting into the sandwich jig.*

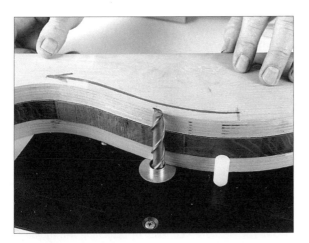

6-50. *The router cutting the sandwiched workpiece. The bottom pattern contacts the guide bushing in the router-table plate.*

6-51. *Standard curved molding has been used on this grandfather clock.*

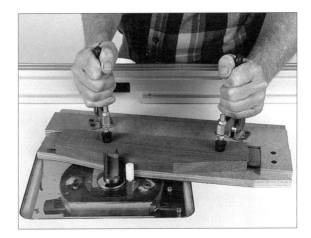

6-52. *This jig is designed to cut half a curve for a chair back. This jig should be used with a starting pin shown to the left of the router bit. The bearing on the bottom of the cutter contacts the jig.*

The standard procedure consists of cutting the piece to its rough shape on the band saw and then using the router or shaper to smooth the piece. This is the safest way to proceed because the woodworker is working with a large piece of wood. Then the molding is cut off the larger piece. If the molding is curved, the finished edge should be cut off using the single-point technique described on page 85 and shown in 6-53.

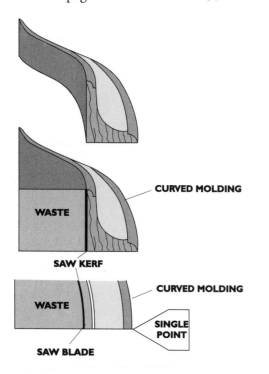

6-53. *The side detail on the molding. First the molding is made, and then it is cut off with a band-saw using the single-point technique.*

Start by making an accurate half-pattern of the curve out of plywood. Then use the half-pattern to create a full-pattern. A full-pattern is required because the two pieces of molding required are mirror images of each other and can't be made efficiently from a simple half-pattern. When making patterns, always extend the curves beyond the finished ends of the workpiece so that the starter pin contacts the pattern before

the cutter actually cuts into the molding. This provides the woodworker with more control.

Next, screw the half-pattern to the full-pattern and saw out the pattern. Trim the pattern using a flush-trim bit on the router table (6-54).

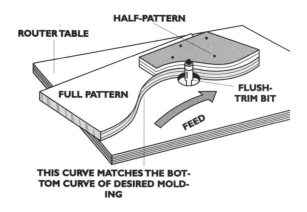

6-54. *Making curved molding using a jig. The first step consists of making a half-pattern slightly longer than required. Then a full pattern for the molding is made from the half-pattern. The full-sized pattern is sawn out and smoothed with a flush-trim bit.*

Now, using screws attach the two moldings to the full-pattern (6-55). Because the molding will be glued to the front of the cabinet, these screw holes will never show. Next, screw a piece of the same material to the opposite side of the full

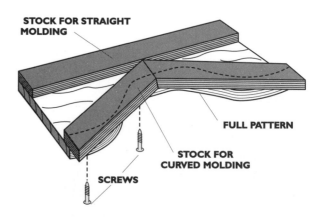

6-55. *The next step consists of attaching the molding stock to the pattern with screws. The grain of the workpiece should run parallel to the pattern's edge.*

template. This will be the molding needed on the clock or cabinet sides. This allows the woodworker to shape the straight molding with the same bit setup used for the curved molding, which guarantees that the two moldings will fit properly at the corner. It also serves to keep the pattern level on the router table.

Next, cut the molding to its general size and shape by pattern-sawing it as described and illustrated in Pattern-Sawing on pages 127 and 128 and shown in 6-56 and 6-57. Then pattern-rout the curved pieces and the straight stock with a flush-trim bit to produce a smooth surface without a shaped edge (6-58).

The next step consists of shaping the edge with a router or shaper to create the molding. Depending on the profile and the bits available, the bit can be guided with either a ball bearing or with a pointed follower. In either case, the ball bearing or follower runs along the edge of the template. If a pointed follower is being used, its underside should be relieved to provide clearance for the bit.

Always start the cut by pivoting the pattern against the starting pin (6-59). Remember that

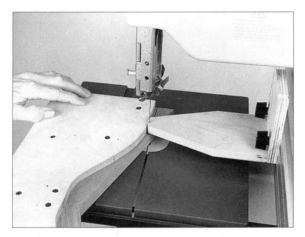

6-56. *The third step consists of pattern-sawing the molding on the band saw. Then it is routed flush to the pattern with a flush-trim bit.*

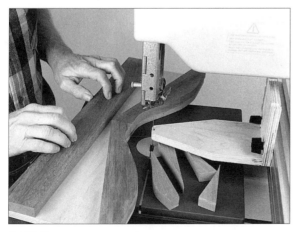

6-57. *Pattern-sawing technique.*

6-58. *Pattern-routing the curved pieces.*

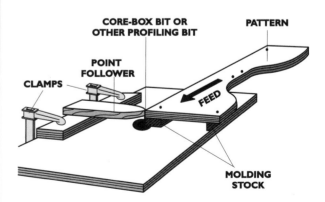

6-59. *Next, the edges of the moldings are routed with either a bit with a ball bearing or with a point follower, as shown here.*

when the molding is being routed, that part of the cut will be made against the grain.

After the profiles have been routed, unscrew the molding from the template. Next, cut the molding off the waste using the single-point method discussed on page 85. Clamp a single-point follower to the band-saw table with the point aligned with the front of the blade. The distance between the blade and the follower determines the width of the molding. The curved face of the molding contacts the point during the cut. When a point follower is being used, the curved side of the molding should be kept perpendicular to the follower (6-60).

The final step consists of sanding the molding opposite the curved edge. This is easily done with a sanding drum in a drill press using the same point-following technique (6-61 and 6-62).

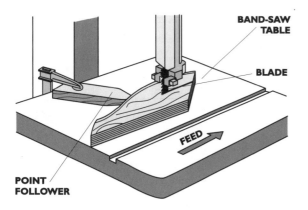

6-60. Now, the molding is unscrewed and the band saw is used to remove the waste. A point follower should be used to guide the cut.

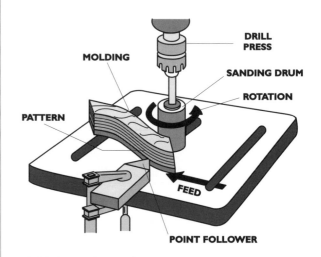

6-61. In the final step, the band-sawed side of the cut is sanded using a single-point follower on the drill press.

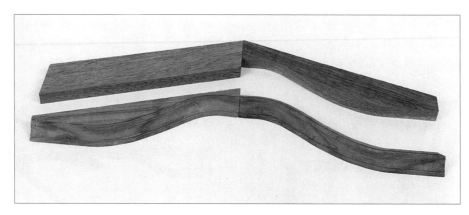

6-62. Curved molding pieces.

CHAPTER 7 Safety Techniques

The band saw is a popular tool because it is easy to use and is so versatile. It is also relatively safe to use because the blade is small compared to blades on other tools and it cannot "kick back" as can blades on other tools, but safety can only be ensured if the proper precautions are taken. Read the follow safety rules carefully. Observe each and every one.

1. Read the instruction manual that comes with the saw before operating it.

2. If still not thoroughly familiar with the operation of the band saw after reading the instruction manual and the information in this book, get advice from a qualified person.

3. Make sure that the machine is properly grounded, and that the wiring codes are followed.

4. Do not operate the band saw while under the influence of drugs, alcohol, or medication, or if tired.

5. Always wear eye protection (safety glasses or a face shield) and hearing protection (ear plugs).

6. Wear a dust mask. Long-term exposure to the fine dust created by the band saw is not healthy.

7. Remove ties, rings, watches, and all jewelry. Shirtsleeves should be rolled up. This is to prevent anything from getting caught in the saw.

8. Make sure that the guards are in place, and use them at all times. The guards protect band-saw users from coming into contact with the blade.

9. Make sure that the saw-blade teeth point downward toward the table.

10. Adjust the upper blade guard so that it is no more than about ¼ inch above the material being cut.

11. Make sure that the blade has been properly tensioned and tracked, and that it is the proper size and type for the job at hand.

12. When folding and unfolding blades, be especially careful. Blades have a lot of spring. Hold the blade away from the body. Wear gloves and eye protection.

13. Stop the band saw before removing scrap pieces from the table.

14. Always keep hands and fingers away from the blade.

15. Hold the workpiece firmly against the table. Do not attempt to saw stock that does not have a flat surface unless a suitable support is being used.

16. Use a push stick for the last inch or two of a cut. This is the most dangerous time because the cut is complete and the blade is exposed. Lay the push stick on the table and then pick it up and use it. Push sticks are commercially available.

17. Hold the wood firmly and feed it into the blade at a moderate speed.

18. Turn off the machine if the material has to be backed out of an uncompleted or jammed cut.

Glossary

Adjustable Taper Jig A taper-cutting jig with a hinge on one end and a locking mechanism on the opposite end that can be adjusted to the desired angle. Refer to Cutting Tapers on pages 105 to 107.

Alternate-Set Blades Blades that have every other tooth bent in the same direction. These types of blades give the smoothest cut. Refer to Blades with Different Tooth Sets on page 39.

Band Saw A saw blade in the form of an endless steel blade or band with teeth on one side that rotates around two or more wheels.

Barrel Cut A condition in which the blade flexes sideways in the workpiece, making a curved cut. Refer to Tensioning Principles on pages 46 to 48.

Beam Strength The ability of a band-saw blade to resist deflection.

Bevel Cuts Cuts made with the band-saw table tilted. Refer to Bevel Cuts on page 104.

Bi-Metal Blades Blades with hard teeth and relatively soft bodies. The teeth are composed of a piece of cobalt steel that is laminated to the body. Refer to Blade-Hardness Characteristics and Metal Composition on pages 53 to 57.

Blade Width The measurement from the back of the blade to the front.

Book-Matching The technique of resawing two pieces and then gluing them together. Refer to Resawing on pages 101 to 104.

Carbon Blades Blades that have more carbon content than do spring-steel blades. These blades, usually black, have much harder teeth than spring-steel blades. Refer to Blade-Hardness Characteristics and Metal Composition on pages 53 to 57.

Compound-Sawn Pattern A pattern that is sawn from two adjacent sides of the workpiece. Refer to Determining Which Type of Pattern to Use on pages 124 to 126.

Corner Rotation Point A jig used with circle-cutting jigs to remove a quarter-circle of waste. Refer to Corner Rotation Points on page 139.

Crosscut A cut made across the grain of the workpiece. Refer to Crosscutting on pages 96 to 98 .

Cut-and-Glue Scroll-Sawing The technique of cutting two halves of one piece and then gluing them together. It is done to allow a narrow blade to make inside cuts. Refer to page 93.

Depth-of-Cut Capacity The thickest cut that a band saw can make.

Double-Pattern A pattern used twice on an object when the object has the same profile from two adjacent sides. A double-pattern would be used on a project such as a cabriole leg. Refer to Determining Which Type of Pattern to Use on pages 124 to 126.

Dovetail Joint An extremely strong two-part joint that consists of a tail and a mating pin. Dovetail joints are made with a series of angled cuts. A taper jig and a series of spacer blocks can be used to make these cuts. Refer to Making Dovetails with Spacing Blocks on pages 110 to 122.

File Band A flexible band to which short pieces of file are attached. It is used for industrial purposes. Refer to Special-Purpose Blades on pages 44 to 45.

Filing The traditional method for sharpening a band-saw blade in which the teeth are sharpened with a file. Refer to Sharpening Blades on pages 63 to 65.

Fixed-Angle Taper Jig An angled piece of wood with a brass piece in one end that pushes the work-piece through the end when tapered pieces are being cut. Refer to Cutting Tapers on pages 105 to 107.

Fixture A store-bought or user-made accessory that positions or holds the work. Refer to Making and Using Jigs and Fixtures on pages 129 to 148.

Flexible-Back Carbon Blades Carbon blades with soft, flexible backs. These blades have hard, durable teeth. Refer to Blade-Hardness Character-istics and Metal Composition on pages 53 to 57.

Form The shape of the band-saw blade teeth. Refer to Tooth Form and Set on page 38.

Foundry Band A very thick blade or band that is used to cut waste off castings. Refer to Special-Purpose Blades on pages 43 to 45.

Friction Band A blade or band designed to cut composite metals on very large saws. Refer to Spe-cial-Purpose Blades on pages 43 to 45.

Friction-Sawing A metal-cutting technique in which the blade runs up to 15,000 FPM. This technique is used to cut hard materials such as grat-ings, screens, and high-strength steels.

Full-Pattern The entire shape of the object that is used when the object is not symmetrical, that is, that its proportions are not balanced. Refer to Determining Which Type of Pattern to Use on pages 124 to 126.

Furniture Band A blade or band that usually has hard edges and a flexible back that is used by furni-ture manufacturers to cut contours and shapes. Refer to Special-Purpose Blades on pages 43 to 45.

Guide Post A moveable post to which the top guide assembly is attached that is raised or lowered to accommodate different thickness of wood. Refer to Guide Assembly on page 28.

Hard-Back Carbon Blades Carbon blades with hard backs that allow the blade to tolerate the high tension used for metal-cutting. Refer to Blade-Hardness Characteristics and Metal Composition on pages 53 to 57.

Harmonic Vibration A condition caused by factors such as blade speed, tension, feed pressure, etc., in which the blade vibrates. Harmonic vibra-tion can shorten blade life.

Hook-Tooth Blade An aggressive-cutting blade that has a positive rake angle and the fewest num-ber of teeth of band-saw blades. Refer to Types of Blades with Different Forms on page 38.

Intarsia A technique in which two different solid-wood designs are used next to each other as a decorative motif. Refer to Intarsia and Marquetry Techniques on pages 90 and 91.

Jig A store-bought or user-made accessory that positions or holds the work and also guides the tool. Refer to Making and Using Jigs and Fixtures on pages 129 to 148.

Knife Band A band that doesn't have teeth, but instead has a straight blade, scallop, or wavy edges. Knife bands give a clean cut without creating sawdust or waste. Refer to Special-Purpose Blades on pages 43 to 45.

Lead A blade's tendency to pull to one side. Refer to Indications of a Poorly Tensioned Blade on pages 47 and 48.

Marquetry A technique in which two different veneer designs are used next to each other as a decorative motif. Refer to Intarsia and Marquetry Techniques on pages 90 and 91.

Mortise-and-Tenon Joint An extremely strong two-part joint is which a slot (mortise) is cut into one piece and a mating piece (tenon) fits into the slot. Refer to Making Mortise-and-Tenon Joints on pages 108 to110.

Nibbling The technique often used on tight curves in which the blade is used to remove small pieces of material so that the workpiece can be rotated without having to twist the blade body. Refer to Nibbling on page 88.

Pantograph A mechanical device used to change the size of patterns. It consists of a follower point that is guided along the original design, and a pencil point that automatically recreates the outline in its exact proportions in a desired size. Refer to Changing the Sizes of Patterns on pages 123 and 124.

Pattern A drawing of the desired shape that is placed on top of the workpiece and cut out. Refer to Patterns and Templates on pages 123 to 128.

Pattern-Routing The technique of smoothing a shape that has been pattern-sawn by attaching a template to the workpiece and using a flush-trim router bit to remove the waste. Refer to Pattern-Routing Jigs on pages 142 to 148.

Pattern-Sanding The technique of using a sanding drum on a drill press to smooth patterns. Refer to Pattern-Sanding Jigs on page 140.

Pitch The size of the teeth on the blade, usually given as a number that indicates how many teeth are in one inch of blade (TPI). Refer to Pitch on pages 36 and 37.

Ply-Core Band A band or blade with coarse teeth and a flexible back that is designed specifically to cut plywood. Refer to Special-Purpose Blades on pages 43 to 45.

Polishing Band A band used to polish objects. A platen usually holds the band in place. Refer to Special-Purpose Blades on pages 43 to 45.

Quarter-Pattern A pattern that has one quarter of the shape of the object. A quarter-pattern is used when the object has four corners that are the same, such as in the case of an oval shape. Refer to Determining Which Type of Pattern to Use on pages 124 to 126.

Radius Cut A cut made in the corner of the workpiece. This cut forms a quarter-circle. Refer to Quarter-Circle Jigs on pages 137 and 138.

Raker-Set Blades Blades with group of teeth that are alternately set in opposite directions.

Release Cut A cut made to meet with the end of a long cut that is used to prevent situations in which the workpiece cannot be retracted from the blade. Refer to Release Cuts on pages 85 and 86.

Resawing The technique of cutting a thick board in half along its width. Refer to Resawing on pages 101 to 104.

Rip Cut A cut made with the grain of the wood. Refer to Rip Cuts on pages 98 to 100.

Round Band A band that can be used to cut from all directions, not just the front. These bands can only be used on specially designed band saws. Refer to Special-Purpose Blades on pages 43 to 45.

Sanding Band An accessory for consumer-grade band saws that is used to smooth wood. Refer to Special-Purpose Blades on pages 43 to 45.

Sandwich Jig A jig that holds the workpiece between two identical patterns. This jig allows the entire assembly to be flipped over whenever the grain changes direction. Refer to Pattern-Routing Jigs on pages 142 to 148.

Scroll-Sawing The technique of using narrow blades to make tight turns. Refer to Scroll-Sawing on pages 92 and 93.

Set The bend of a band-saw blade's teeth. Refer to Tooth Form and Set on pages 38 to 40.

Skip-Tooth Blade A blade that has every other tooth missing. This type of blade has a coarse pitch and cuts much faster than other types of blades. Refer to Types of Blades with Different Forms on pages 38 to 40.

Spring-Steel Blades Blades, usually silver, that are made of spring steel. These types of blades are not very hard. Refer to Blade-Hardness Characteristics and Metal Composition on pages 53 to 57.

Stack-Sawing The technique of sandwiching multiple pieces together and cutting them. Refer to Making Multiple Pieces on pages 95 and 96.

Standard-Tooth Blade A blade with teeth that are spaced closely together. Refer to Types of Blades with Different Forms on pages 36 to 40.

Step Taper Jig A jig that has three notches or steps and is used to make tapers on one side, oppo-site sides, or adjacent sides of a workpiece. Refer to Cutting Tapers on pages 105 to 107.

Tapers Angled cuts made along the grain of the workpiece. Refer to Cutting Tapers on pages 105 to 107.

Templates Patterns made out of durable material such as plywood, plastic, or Masonite. Refer to Patterns and Templates on pages 123 to 128.

Thrust Bearings Round bearings on the wheel that are used to stop the rearward movement of the blade. Refer to Guide Assembly on page 28.

Tracking The act of positioning or balancing the blade on the wheels. There are two types of tracking: Center-tracking and coplanar-tracking. Center-tracking consists of tilting the top wheel, usually rearwards, until the blade tracks in the center of the top wheel. Coplanar tracking consists of balancing wider blades by aligning the wheels. Refer to Tracking the Blade on pages 68 to 77.

Turning Holes Holes drilled in key positions in the workpiece to ensure that the waste piece can be easily separated from the workpiece or to give the operator more space in which to rotate the workpiece around the blade. Refer to Turning Holes on page 86.

Variable-Pitch Blade A blade with variable or wavy set which helps to decrease vibration caused by the running blade. Refer to Variable-Pitch Blades on page 36.

V-block A simple fixture that is clamped to the rip fence. This fixture performs the same tasks that a tilting table performs. Refer to V-Block Fixture on page 129.

Wandering Cut A condition in which the blade, not sufficiently tensioned, flexes as it cuts and "wanders." Refer to Indications of a Poorly Tensioned Blade on pages 47 and 48.

Welding The process of attaching a broken blade. Refer to Welding Blades on pages 59 and 60.

METRIC EQUIVALENTS CHART

INCHES TO MILLIMETERS AND CENTIMETERS

MM— Millimeters   CM—Centimeters

Inches	MM	CM	Inches	CM	Inches	CM
⅛	3	0.3	9	22.9	30	76.2
¼	6	0.6	10	25.4	31	78.7
⅜	10	1.0	11	27.9	32	81.3
½	13	1.3	12	30.5	33	83.8
⅝	16	1.6	13	33.0	34	86.4
¾	19	1.9	14	35.6	35	88.9
⅞	22	2.2	15	38.1	36	91.4
1	25	2.5	16	40.6	37	94.0
1¼	32	3.2	17	43.2	38	96.5
1½	38	3.8	18	45.7	39	99.1
1¾	44	4.4	19	48.3	48	101.6
2	51	5.1	20	50.8	41	104.1
2½	64	6.4	21	53.3	42	106.7
3	76	7.6	22	55.9	43	109.2
3½	89	8.9	23	58.4	44	111.8
4	102	10.2	24	61.0	45	114.3
4½	114	11.4	25	63.5	46	116.8
5	127	12.7	25	66.0	47	119.4
6	152	15.2	27	68.6	48	121.9
7	178	17.8	28	71.1	49	124.5

Index